CHARLES THE GREAT

CHARLES THE GREAT

BY

THOMAS HODGKIN, D.C.L.

KENNIKAT PRESS
Port Washington, N. Y./London

CHARLES THE GREAT

First published in 1897
Reissued in 1970 by Kennikat Press
Library of Congress Catalog Card No: 71-112808
ISBN 0-8046-1075-4

Manufactured by Taylor Publishing Company   Dallas, Texas

PREFACE

In attempting to compress the history of the great Emperor Charles within the narrow limits of the present volume, I have undertaken a difficult task, and I trust that my fellow-historians will consider, not how much has been omitted, but how much, or rather how little, it was possible to insert.

It may be thought that I might have gained space by proceeding at once to the beginning of Charles's own reign, instead of devoting more than eighty pages to his predecessors, but this did not seem to me possible. The great Emperor was the last term of an ascending series —nobles, mayors of the palace, kings; and in order to understand the law of the series it is absolutely necessary to study some of its earlier members.

It will be observed that, though I generally speak of my hero as Charles, I have not absolutely declined to use the familiar compound Charlemagne. This is done with no disrespect to the teaching of my honoured friend, the late Prof. Freeman, who first lifted up his voice against this form of the name. A generation ago his protest against Gallicising the great Teutonic hero was certainly needed, but now that the lesson has been learnt, I think that we need not absolutely ban a form of his name which has been used by Milton and by Scott, and which, after all, by its union of the Teutonic Karl with the Latin Magnus, not inaptly symbolises the blending of German and Roman elements in the Frankish Empire.

A few words as to our authorities. For the period before the accession of Pippin our chief authority is the chronicle which is known by the name of *Fredegarius*, very meagre, and written in barbarous Latin, but honest; then a still more miserable continuation of this work by an unknown scribe; and lastly, a much better performance, from a literary point of view, *The Lives of the Bishops of Metz*, by Paulus Diaconus.

For the reigns of Pippin and of Charles the Great we have fairly satisfactory materials in the shape of the Annals, which now began to be kept at various monasteries; chief among them the *Annales Laurissenses majores*, so-called from their connection, real or supposed, with the great monastery of Lorsch (in Hesse-Darmstadt, about ten miles east of Worms). So extensive, however, is the knowledge of State affairs possessed by this writer that it is the opinion of Professor Ranke, and of most modern enquirers, that he cannot have been a mere monk writing his chronicle in a convent, but that we have here in fact the chronicles of the Frankish kingdom. This view is to some extent confirmed by the fact that there is a fuller recension of them in a more literary form, which bears the name of *Annales Einhardi*, and thus professes to be the work of Charles's friend and secretary. The precious *Vita Caroli*, from the pen of the same writer, is described in the following pages.

The writers who in modern times have treated of the life of Charles the Great number some hundreds, and I make no pretension to even a superficial acquaintance with the bibliography of so vast a subject, but I may mention that the books which I have found most helpful in the composition of the following pages are Waitz's *Deutsche Verfassungsgeschichte*, Guizot's *Lectures on the History of Civilisation*, Dahn's *Urgeschichte der germanischen und romanischen Völker*, and pre-eminently the series of *Jahrbücher der deutschen Geschichte*, in which Bonnell has treated of *The Beginnings of the Carolingian House;* Oelsner, of *The Life of Pippin, King of the Franks;* and Abel and Simson, of *The Life of Charles the Great*. To the last work (in two volumes) I have been under great and continual obligation.

THOS. HODGKIN.

CONTENTS

CHAPTER I

CHAPTER VII

CHAPTER VIII

CHAPTER IX

CHAPTER X

CHAPTER XI

CHAPTER XII

CHAPTER XIII

CHAPTER I

INTRODUCTION

In the gradual transformation of the old world of classical antiquity into the world with which the statesmen of to-day must deal, no man played a greater part than Charles the Great, King of the Franks and Emperor of Rome. The sharp lines of demarcation which we often draw between period and period, and which are useful as helps to memory, have not for the most part had any real existence in history, for in the world of men, as in the development of the material universe, it is true that uniformity rather than cataclysm is the rule : *Natura non vadit per saltum.* Still there are some great landmarks, such as the foundation of Constantinople, Alaric's capture of Rome, the Hegira of Mohammed, the discovery of America, the Reformation, and the French Revolution, which have no merely artificial existence. We can see that the thoughts of the great majority of civilised men were suddenly forced into a different channel by such events, that after they had occurred, men hoped for other benefits and feared other dangers than they had looked for before these events took place. And such a changeful moment in the history of the world was undoubtedly the life of the great ruler who is generally spoken of as Charlemagne, and pre-eminently the year 800, when he was crowned as Emperor at Rome.

When Charles appeared upon the scene, the Roman Empire—at least as far as Western Europe was concerned — had been for more than three centuries slowly dying. An event, to which allusion has just been made—the capture of Rome by Alaric in 410—had dealt the great world-empire a mortal blow, and yet so tough was its constitution, so deeply was the thought engraven even on the hearts of its most barbarous enemies, "Rome is the rightful mistress of the world," that it seemed as if that world-empire could not die. The Visigoth, the Ostrogoth, the Vandal, the Burgundian, the Lombard, coming forth from the immemorial solitude of their forests, streamed over the cities and the vineyards of the Mediterranean lands, and erected therein their rude state-systems, their barbaric sovereignties; but even in framing their uncouth national codes they were forced to use the language of Rome; in government they could not dispense with the official machinery of the Empire; in religious affairs, above all, they found themselves always face to face with men to whom the city by the Tiber was still *Roma caput mundi.* Hence in all these new barbarian kingdoms that arose on the ruins of the Empire there was a certain feeling of precariousness and unrest, a secret fear that the power which had come into being so strangely and so unexpectedly would in a moment vanish away, and that the Roman Augustus would assert himself once more as supreme over the nations; to borrow a phrase from the controversies of a much later date, the Visigothic and Burgundian and Lombard kings were obviously kings *de facto ;* but there was a latent consciousness in the minds of their subjects, perhaps in their own also, that they were not kings *de jure.*

Had the Italian peninsula been less easily accessible by way of the Julian Alps, or had Rome been situated in as strong a position as Constantinople, it is possible that this secret belief in her rightful predominance might have won back for a Roman emperor that dominion over Europe which was in fact wielded for a time by the Roman popes. But the virtual transference of the seat of empire from the Tiber to the Bosphorus, which was the result of the foundation of the new Rome, and the frequent successful sieges of the old Rome, prevented the Roman emperor from thus reasserting himself. There were jealousies between Rome and Constantinople already before the end of the fourth century, and when under Justinian the Empire made its wonderful efforts to recover the ground which it had lost in Africa, in Italy, and in Spain, though these reconquests were effected in the name of a Roman Augustus, it was felt, and often loudly asserted, that the armies which fought under the imperial standards were Greek rather than Roman. Thus, through all the kingdoms of the west, even while the emperor enthroned at Constantinople was looked upon as in some sense the legitimate monarch of the world, the old deep-rooted hostility between East and West also made itself felt, and it was becoming every day more improbable that the western lands should ever be brought under the rule of a "Byzantine" Cæsar.

Ere the long, slow agony which I have called the death of Rome was completed, the world was startled by that outbreak of fierce Semitic monotheism which is associated with the name of Mohammed.   In 622, rather more than two centuries after Alaric's capture of Rome, Mohammed escaped from Mecca to Medina, and in this retreat of his the followers of his faith in succeeding ages have rightly seen the beginning of his career of spiritual conquest, wherefore they date all their events from the midnight journey of a fugitive, even as the other great Oriental faith has taken for its landmark the birth of a little child in a stable.   Before Mohammed's death in 632 the career of Saracen conquest had begun. Ere the close of the seventh century Syria, Persia, Egypt, North Africa, were torn from the empire of the Cæsars and obeyed the rule of the Caliph.   In 711 Europe saw the first breach made in its defences when the great Iberian peninsula (all save a few mountain glens in the remote north) was conquered by the Moors, and Mecca took the place of Jerusalem or Rome as the spiritual centre of gravity for Spain.   The turbaned invaders crossed the Pyrenees ; in 725 they penetrated as far as Autun, only 150 miles from Paris.   Though defeated by Charles Martel, the grandfather of Charlemagne, in the great battle of Poitiers, the Moors remained encamped on the soil of that which we now call France. Narbonne was in their possession at the time of the birth of Charlemagne, and remained so during the years of his boyhood, till won back for Christendom by his father in 759.

In the east of Europe the Avars still hung menacingly over the Italian and Illyrian lands.   A people allied to

524 and 534, his sons conquered Burgundy, and thus added to their father's kingdom the whole valley of the Rhone from its source to its mouth, except the narrow but rich land of Provence, which was retained by the Ostrogothic kings of Italy for a few years longer, but in 536 this also became Frankish. Contemporaneously with the conquest of Burgundy proceeded the conquest of Thuringia, the fair region in the heart of Germany which still bears that name, and the establishment of the over-lordship of the Franks over the nation of the Bavarians, whose country stretched from the Danube across the Alps, into the valley of the Adige and up to the very gates of Italy. The date of this last addition to the Frankish dominions cannot be precisely ascertained, but may be stated approximately at the year 535.

It will be seen from this brief summary how rapidly the tide of Frankish conquest rose almost to the same high-water mark which it maintained at the time of the birth of Charlemagne. In fifty years from the first appearance of Clovis as a warrior, the Franks have subdued the whole of modern France (except a little strip of Languedoc), the Low Countries, Switzerland, and all Germany as far as the Elbe and the mountains of Bohemia, except Hanover and a part of Westphalia which is occupied by the untamed and still heathen Saxons. Such a monarchy even now would be the greatest power in Europe. In the sixth century, with Spain weakened by the estrangement between Arians and Catholics, with Italy torn by strife between the Empire and its barbarian occupants, with Britain still in utter chaos, nibbled at but not devoured by her

Anglo-Saxon invaders, the kingdom of the Franks, when united and at peace within itself, was the strongest power in Europe, with the two doubtful exceptions of the kingdom of the savage Avars and the tottering fabric of the Roman Empire.

But the years in which the Frankish kingdom was thus united and at peace with itself were few. It had been built up by the ferocious energy of one man and his sons; it was hardly in any true sense of the word national, and he and his descendants treated it as an estate rather than as a country, partitioned and repartitioned it in a way which wasted its strength and ruined its chances of attaining to political unity. The comparison may seem a strange one, but in the personal, non-national character of his policy the first Frankish king reminds one of the latest French conqueror; the career of Clovis may be illustrated by that of Napoleon. Both men emphatically "fought for their own hands"; both were more intent on massing great countries under their sway than on really assimilating the possessions which they had already acquired; both in different ways made, or tried to make, the Catholic Church an instrument of their ambition; and both seem to have looked upon Europe, or so much of it as they could acquire, as a big estate to be divided among their children or relations.

There is no need here to dwell upon the perplexing details of the division of the kingdom of Clovis among his sons and grandsons. We perceive a tendency to regard the north-eastern portion of the realm, especially that conquered from Syagrius, as the true kernel of the kingdom; and therefore, widely as the dominions of

the brothers stretch asunder, their capitals, Metz,
Orleans, Soissons, Paris, all lie comparatively near to
one another, all probably within the ring-fence of the
Syagrian kingdom. But there is also a tendency to
fall asunder into four great divisions. Burgundy and
Aquitaine, though they do not formally resume their
independence, are often seen as separate kingdoms
under a Frankish king. But the more important
division, the more fateful rivalry separates the two
northern kingdoms, which eventually receive the names
of Neustria and Austrasia. In Neustria, which contained the regions of Flanders, Normandy, Champagne,
and Central France as far as the Loire, there was
doubtless a very large Gallo-Roman population, though
its numbers may not have so enormously preponderated
over those of the Teutonic immigrants as in Aquitaine
and Burgundy. The Roman language and some remains
of Roman culture survived here in Neustria, and were
preparing the ground for the formation of the mediæval
kingdom of France. Austrasia, on the other hand, the
territory of the Rhine and the Moselle, seems to have
remained essentially German. The Latin speech in
this country must have been confined to ecclesiastics
and a few of the more cultivated courtiers; it can
never have been the speech of the people. And
though here we must speak rather by conjecture than
by proof, it is probable that the old Germanic institutions
of the hundred and the *gau* survived here in greater
vigour than on the alien soil of the Romanised Gaul.
It was also through the rulers of Austrasia that the
connection, frail and precarious as it often might be,
was kept up between the Frankish monarchy and the

great semi-independent duchies of the Thuringians, the Alamanni, and the Bavarians.

Thus already in the fissure between the western and eastern portions of the Merovingian kingdom we see the rift, premonitory of that mighty chasm which now separates the great states of France and Germany.

CHAPTER II

EARLY MAYORS OF THE PALACE

THE historical student who visits in thought the nursery of modern European states—the period from 500 to 800 of the Christian era—finds with amused surprise how many of the features familiar to him in their weather-beaten old age he can trace in the faces of those baby kingdoms. Gothic Spain, with its manifold councils, its ecclesiastical intolerance, and its bitter persecutions of the Jews, is the anticipation of the Spain of the Ferdinands and the Philips. Italy, cleft in sunder by the patrimony of St. Peter and with the undying hostility between the pope and the Lombard king, presages the very conflict which is now being waged between the Vatican and the Quirinal. England, notwithstanding all her early elements of confusion and mismanagement, clings desperately to her one great saving institution of the Witan, and thus travails in birth with the future parliament.

And even so, France under the Merovingian kings is the land of centralised government, which though strong and imposing in theory, repeatedly shows itself weak and insufficient in practice from the incapacity of the governing brain to perform the manifold functions assigned to it by destiny. As far as we can see, Clovis and his immediate successors wielded a power which was practically unlimited. The checks which the German nations from the time of Tacitus downwards had imposed on the authority of their kings had almost entirely disappeared before the overmastering power of the great Salian chief who had united the whole of Gaul under his sway, and who was continually reminded by his friends, the Christian bishops, how high had been the throne and how heavy the sceptre of the Roman Augustus in that very region. The well-known story of the vase of Soissons illustrates at once the German memories of freedom and the Merovingian mode of establishing a despotism. As a battle comrade the Frankish warrior protests against Clovis receiving an ounce beyond his due share of the spoils. As a battle leader Clovis rebukes his henchman for the dirtiness of his accoutrements, and cleaves his skull to punish him for his independence.

There can be little doubt that it was the influence of Roman and ecclesiastical ideas which tended to exalt the rude chiefs of the Salian tribe into their later position of practically despotic monarchs, surrounded by a crowd of fawning flatterers and servile courtiers. The effect of this exaltation on the royal house itself was disastrous. Merovingian royalty flowered too soon and faded early. Clovis himself was short-lived, dying, as we have seen, at the age of five-and-forty. But two or three generations later the career of the kings, his descendants, was of far more portentous brevity. Nothing is more common than to find a

Merovingian king who is a father at fifteen, or even earlier, and who dies (not always by a violent death) under thirty. Let us take a few of the lives of the later kings as an illustration. Dagobert I., who is a sort of patriarch among them, dies at thirty-eight; his son, Clovis II., at twenty-four; of the sons of this latter king, Chlothair III. dies at eighteen, Childeric II. at twenty. Theodoric III. actually lives to the age of thirty-eight, but of his sons one dies at thirteen and another at eighteen. And so on with many other names that might be quoted. It was evidently by their vices that these hapless "do-nothing" kings were hurried to such early graves. Every student of the pages of Gregory of Tours knows the dreary picture of morals and of social life which is there presented : the coarseness of the barbarian without his rough fidelity, the voluptuousness of the Gallo-Roman noble without his culture. Even as we see at the present day in the contact of two civilisations or of two faiths, notably in the contact of Christianity and Mohammedanism, that the men whose position places them on the borders of the two are apt to display the vices of both and the virtues of neither, so was it with the Frankish nobles and bishops of Gaul in the sixth and seventh centuries, and so emphatically was it with their head, the Frankish king who reigned at Metz or Orleans or Paris. Immersed in his swinish pleasures, with his constitution ruined by his early excesses, what could the sickly youth, the Childebert or Chlothair of the day, do to overtake the mass of business which the administration of the realm, with its highly centralised mechanism, imposed upon him? He could not do it all, and in practice he did nothing, and sank easily, perhaps happily, into the condition of a *roi fainéant.* Dagobert I., who died in 638, is the last Merovingian king who displays some royal energy and strength of purpose. After him for more than a century a series of pageant kings pass before us, Clovises and Theodorics and Chilperics, whose names history refuses to remember, but whose pitiable condition is represented to us by a few vivid touches from the hand of Einhard, the biographer of Charlemagne. He describes to us how the Merovingian king, seated in his chair of state, received the ambassadors of foreign powers, and repeated, parrot-like, the answers which he had been taught to give; how he travelled through the land in a waggon drawn by a yoke of oxen, with a clownish herdsman for his charioteer, and thus made his appearance when his presence was required at the palace or at the yearly assemblies of the people; but how for the greater part of the year he abode at one small villa in the country, living on its produce, eked out by a scanty grant from his prime minister, and having in truth nothing that he could call his own save his royal title, his long flowing hair, and his pendulous beard, which were the marks of his kingly state.

Doubtless it is not only the constitutional sovereign who is obliged to content himself with only a small share of actual power. The despot also, if he wishes to have any enjoyment of life, must leave much to be done by his ministers, who, whatever show of deference they may yield to his judgment, will practically decide for themselves the great mass of administrative questions that come before them. Thus Louis XIII. had his Richelieu; thus the Sultan of Turkey has his Grand

Vizier; thus, till our own day, the Mikado of Japan had his Shogun, whom European travellers wrote about by his Chinese title of Tycoon. The relation of these last regents to the royal dynasty in whose name they ruled for many centuries, while depriving them of every shred of actual power, seems to furnish the closest parallel in all history to the relation of the Frankish *major domus* to the Merovingian king.

The origin and early stages of the growth of the power of the "mayor of the palace" (our usual English translation of the title *major domus*) form one of the most difficult subjects in Frankish history. Perhaps the greatest difficulty is to understand why it is that no Teutonic name of an office which was certainly not Roman but Teutonic should have survived in history. An opinion which has found some powerful supporters is that the office was the same which was called by the Germans *seneschal*, "the oldest servant" in the palace, and that as the last part of this word denoted a servile condition, the more respectful Latin term *major domus* was adopted instead of it. This opinion is, however, as •powerfully opposed, and certainly the fact that both *major domus* and *seniscalcus* are found in the same documents as titles of apparently different offices seems to throw a doubt upon its correctness.

But whatever the origin of the name, it is pretty clear that the mayor of the palace was originally but the chief domestic of the king, he to whom it appertained to order the ceremonies of the court, to rule the royal pages, probably to superintend the repairs of the royal dwelling. Hence not only reigning kings but queens dowager, and even princesses, had their *majores domus*, and it even seems probable that one king might have several mayors, each superintending one of his various palaces. This, however, is only true of the early days of the mayoralty. As chief man of business to an imperfectly educated, care-encumbered, pleasure-loving king, the mayor of the palace took one burden after another off the royal shoulders, and at the same time drew one source of power after another into his own hands. Especially, at a pretty early period of his career, he seems to have acquired the supreme control of the royal treasury, superintending the collection of the taxes, administering the royal domains, eventually acquiring the power of granting those *beneficia* or (as they would be called in the language of a later day) those fiefs, by which on the one hand the royal property was so seriously diminished, but on the other hand the friendship of an important nobleman might, at a crisis of the mayor's fortunes, be so easily secured.

From the first appearance of the *major domus* in Frankish history till the year when the last *major domus* was crowned King of the Franks, thereby absorbing the lower office in the higher, a period of about 170 years intervened, and during that long space of time these anomalous functionaries assume very different shapes and exercise their powers in very different ways. Sometimes, especially in the earlier years of this period, they are the vigorous upholders of the rights of the crown against a turbulent aristocracy, and then the mayor of the palace seems to anticipate Richelieu. Sometimes they appear at the head of the aristocracy and force their way, almost in spite of the king, into the palace from which they take their title, and then they remind us of the Guises and the Condés of a later day. In Neustria and Burgundy no mayor of the palace who arises there succeeds in making his office hereditary. In Austrasia there is a very early tendency towards hereditary succession in the office, and five generations of able men wielding its growing powers become at last in name, as well as in fact, supreme.

It is out of the question to give here any detailed description of the development of the mayoralty of the palace during that space of nearly two centuries, but one or two illustrations drawn from the history of the times may show what manner of men the mayors were, and how they wielded their power.

"In the tenth year of the reign of Theodoric II., King of Burgundy," says the unlettered chronicler who goes by the name of Fredegarius, "at the instigation of Brunechildis, and by order of Theodoric, Protadius is appointed mayor of the palace, a man of great cleverness and energy in all that he undertook, but fierce was his injustice against private persons. Straining too far the rights of the treasury, he strove to fill it and to enrich himself by ingenious attacks on private property. Wherever he found a man of noble descent, all such he strove to humble, that more might be found who could assume the dignity which he had seized. By these and other exactions, the work of a man too clever for his office, he succeeded in making enemies of all the chief men in Burgundy." The chronicler then goes on to describe how Protadius stirred up strife between Theodoric and his brother Theudebert, King of Austrasia, whom he declared to be no true king's son, but son of a gardener by an adulterous intercourse with the queen.

The Burgundian army marched forth and encamped at a place called Caratiacum, but there the king was advised by his *leudes* [retainers] to make peace with Theudebert. Protadius, however, exhorted them one by one to join battle. Theudebert was encamped not far off with his army. Then all the army of Theodoric, finding a suitable opportunity, rushed upon Protadius, saying that it was better that one man should die than that the whole army should be sent into danger. Now Protadius was sitting in the tent of King Theodoric playing at draughts with the arch-physician Peter. And when the army had surrounded him on every side, and Theodoric was held back by his *leudes* to prevent his going thither, he sent Uncilenus to announce to the army his word of command that they should desist from their plots against Protadius. Uncilenus straightway bore to the army this message: 'Thus orders our lord Theodoric, that Protadius be slain.' Rushing in, therefore, and entering the king's tent from all sides with drawn swords, they slay Protadius. Covered with confusion, Theodoric made an involuntary peace with his brother Theudebert, and both armies returned to their own homes.

"After the decease of Protadius in the eleventh year of Theodoric, Claudius is appointed to the office of *major domus*. He was a Roman by descent, a prudent man, a pleasant story-teller, energetic in all things, given to patience, abounding in counsel, learned in letters, full of faith, desiring friendship with all men. Taking warning by the example of those who had gone before him, he bore himself gently and patiently in his high office, but this only hindrance had he, that he was burdened with too great fatness of body.

"In the twelfth year of Theodoric, at the instigation of Brunechildis, Uncilenus, who had by his treacherous words brought about the death of Protadius, had one of his feet cut off, was despoiled of his possessions and reduced to poverty. At the instigation of the same queen, Vulfos, the patrician who had been consenting to the death of Protadius, was killed at the villa of Fauriniacum by order of Theodoric, and Ricomeris, a man of Roman descent, succeeded him in the patriciate."

These events may be taken as a sample of the working of the institution of the *major domus* in Neustria and Burgundy for the greater part of a century. We see a king becoming more and more helpless in the presence of the nobles and clergy whom he and his predecessors have enriched. Theodoric II. is not personally a *fainéant* king, but he cannot prevent murder being committed in his name. We see a *major domus* intent on refilling the royal treasury, and probably not scrupulous as to the means which he employs for that purpose, nor afraid of enriching himself at the same time as his master. We see a grasping and turbulent aristocracy, made up of courtiers and ecclesiastics, who are determined to keep what they have got from the crown, and to whom both the lawful and the lawless acts of the prime minister on behalf of his impoverished master render that minister equally odious. The aristocracy bide their time. When the army is assembled in the field they appeal to the old Teutonic spirit of almost democratic independence, and slay their enemy in defiance of the king's authority. A sleek and supple Gallo-Roman takes the place of the murdered mayor, and in his placid corpulence gives up the struggle, letting things drift as they will. But the vengeance of the palace slumbers not, and in time the aristocratic murderers of the prime minister are themselves cut off by hands as lawless as their own. Such is Merovingian France in the seventh century after Christ.

I have tried to indicate the general character of the *major-domat* in the two western kingdoms of Gaul. In Austrasia, though probably the chief functions of the office are the same, its holder seems to look in a different direction, and certainly arrives at a different end. The Neustrian and Burgundian mayors of the palace are generally striving for the rights of the crown against the aristocracy. In Austrasia they are more often found at the head of the aristocracy and opposed to the crown. In the western kingdoms we see indications that the *major domus* was often a man of humble origin, and that this was part of the grievance of the aristocracy against him. In Austrasia he is generally a man who, by his birth and possessions, takes a foremost place in the realm independently of his official rank. Hence, and from the fact that the office was held in Austrasia by a long succession of able men in the same family, arises the distinction already alluded to that in Austrasia the *major-domat* becomes hereditary, and that it never acquired that character in Neustria.

Lastly—and this difference is perhaps related to most of the others which I have named, as cause is related to effect—the western kingdoms seem at this time to have been always looked on as containing the heart and centre of the Frankish dominion. Thus when a Frankish king had been ruling in Austrasia with Metz for his capital, if by the death of a father or brother he succeeded to the throne of Neustria, he generally migrated westwards to Paris or Soissons, sometimes sending a son or a younger brother to rule in Austrasia, sometimes seeking to rule it from Paris. Now it is clear that there was a strong and growing feeling in Austrasia (which was already beginning to be stirred by some of the same sentiments as the Germany of to-day) that it would not be ruled from Neustria (the ancestress of France). A Merovingian king, the descendant of the Salian Clovis, it would endure, but he must rule, not through Neustrian but through Austrasian instruments. This feeling of national German independence was represented and championed by the mayors of the palace of the line of Arnulf and Pippin, and to their history we now turn.

The ancestors of Charlemagne first emerge into the light of history at the time of the downfall of Queen Brunechildis. No student of Frankish history can ever forget the tragic figure of that queen or her life-long duel with her ignoble and treacherous sister-in-law Fredegundis. While Brunechildis was still in early womanhood (576) came reverses, the murder of her husband, imprisonment, a second marriage, separation from the young husband whom she had so strangely chosen, followed by his death at the bidding of Fredegundis. Meanwhile she returned to Austrasia and ruled there for a time, first in the name of a son, then of a grandson. Driven from thence (600) by the turbulent aristocracy whose power she had striven to quell, she escaped to Burgundy, and governed it for thirteen years in the name of her grandson Theodoric. We have just seen her "instigating" the appointment of Protadius as mayor of the

palace and the punishment of his murderers. All
through these later years of her life the once fascinating
and beautiful woman seems like a lioness at bay. If
Mary, Queen of Scots, had escaped from Fotheringay,
even so could we imagine her, grown grey and hard and
cruel, confronting John Knox and the Scottish lords.
Her grandsons perished early. Theodoric renewed the
war with Theudebert, defeated and slew him, but died
himself at the Austrasian capital in the year 613. And
now were left of the race of Clovis only the four infant
sons of Theodoric II. and their distant relation, Chlothair
of Neustria, son of the hated Fredegundis. War was
inevitable. Which would prevail, the old lioness fighting for her cubs or the whelp of Neustria? At this crisis
the adhesion of two Austrasian nobles to the party of
Chlothair decided the day in his favour. These two
Austrasian nobles were Pippin "of Landen" and Arnulf,
afterwards Bishop of Metz.

Pippin of Landen (so called)[1] had large possessions
in the country between the Meuse and the Moselle,
stretching in an easterly direction toward the Rhine,
including the forest of the Ardennes, and apparently
including also the city of Aquisgranum, which was one day
to be the home of Charlemagne. Pippin was born about
585, and was therefore somewhere about thirty years of
age when war broke out between Brunechildis and
Chlothair. His friend and contemporary, Arnulf, born
of a noble and wealthy Frankish family, had received a

---

[1] It has been shown by Bonnell that neither Pippin of Landen
nor Pippin of Heristal was so called by contemporary writers.
But for the sake of distinction it seems better to retain these
well-known surnames.

better education, apparently, than fell to the lot of most of his class, and, on the recommendation of the "sub-king" Gundulf (possibly mayor of the palace), had been taken into the service of Theudebert, who had assigned to him the government of six provinces. He had married a girl of noble family, by whom he had two sons, Chlodulf and Ansigisel. The latter was the ancestor of Charlemagne.

It was, as we are told, by the secret advice of these two men and other nobles of Austrasia that Chlothair invaded the kingdom. However strong might be their disinclination to the rule of a Neustrian king, their determination not to submit again to "the hateful regimen of a woman," and that woman their old foe Brunechildis, was even stronger. The folly of the old queen, who was at the same time secretly plotting against the life of her Burgundian mayor of the palace, Warnachar, aided their designs. When it came to the decision of battle, the soldiers who should have defended the cause of the young king and his great-grandmother turned their backs without striking a blow. Chlothair had only to pursue and to capture the little princes and their ancestress. One of the princes escaped, and was never heard of more; another was spared as being the godson of Chlothair; two were put to death. The aged Brunechildis was, we are told, tortured for three days by the son of her old rival Fredegundis, led through the camp seated on a camel, then tied by her hair, by one foot and one arm, to a most vicious horse, and dashed to pieces by his furious career. Such were the tender mercies of a Merovingian king.

This first appearance of Pippin and Arnulf on the

stage of history is not a noble one, yet of actual dis-
loyalty or ingratitude they were probably not guilty,
since to Theudebert, the victim of the resentment of
Brunechildis, rather than to the family of Theodoric, his
vanquisher and murderer, they owed allegiance and
gratitude. The subsequent career of the two nobles,
however, is more to their credit. In the year after the
overthrow of Brunechildis, the see of Metz having fallen
vacant, there was a general outcry among the people
that none was so fitted to fill it as Arnulf, the *domesticus*
and *consiliarius* of the king. There was on his part the
usual tearful protestation of unfitness and unwillingness,
but the curtain fell on his acceptance of the episcopal
dignity. His biographer tells the story of his three-
days' fastings, his hair shirt, his boundless hospitality to
poor vagrants, to monks, and to other travellers. We
perceive, however, that he had not wholly lost his
interest in state affairs, for in the year 624 he, with his
friend Pippin, the *major domus*, procured the disgrace
of a certain nobleman named Chrodoald, who was
charged with having abused the king's favour to his
own enrichment and the spoliation of the estates of
other Austrasians. In the next year, too, when Dagobert I., son of Chlothair, who had been sent to rule over
a shorn and diminished Austrasia, met his father near
Paris, and had a sharp contention with him over the
narrow limits of his kingdom, it was Bishop Arnulf who,
at the head of the other bishops and nobles, succeeded
in reconciling father and son.

It seems that Arnulf had for years cherished a desire
to withdraw from the world, but when he mentioned
this project to Dagobert, the young king, who greatly

valued his counsels, was so incensed that he swore that
he would cut off the heads of his two sons if he dared to
leave the court. "My sons' lives," said the intrepid
prelate, "are in the hands of God. Your own life will
not last long if you slay the innocent." On this the
passionate young Merovingian drew his sword, and was
about to attack Arnulf, who, not heeding the wrath of
the king, said, "What are you doing, most miserable of
men? Would you repay evil for good? Here am I
ready for death in obedience to His commands who
gave me life, and who died for me." The nobles
besought the king not to give the bishop the crown of
martyrdom. The queen appeared upon the scene, and
in a few moments she and Dagobert were grovelling at
Arnulf's feet, beseeching forgiveness for the king's
offence, and declaring that he should go when and
whither he would.

So after an episcopate of fifteen years, in 629 Arnulf
retired into the recesses of the Vosges mountains,
accompanied by one friend, Romaric, once a courtier
like himself, who had gone before him into the hermit
life, and who, like him, attained to the honours of saintship.   The death of Arnulf is generally placed in 640, but
we have, in truth, no exact information as to the date.
We only know that Romaric survived him, and that the
body of the now canonised prelate was brought with
great pomp to the city of Metz by order of his successor
in the see, and was there interred in the church of the
Holy Apostles, which has ever since borne his name.

The *Vita Arnulfi*, from which these facts have been
taken, appears to have been the work of a contemporary
(doubtless a much-admiring contemporary), and we need

not therefore here suspect that tendency to flatter
Charlemagne by magnifying the greatness of his
ancestors which has undoubtedly coloured the histories
of some of the members of his family. It is certainly
an interesting fact that a saint should have been the
paternal ancestor, even in the fifth degree, of so great a
statesman as Charlemagne. The standard of mediæval
saintship in the centuries with which we are dealing
was not a high one, but Arnulf's character seems to
have been pure and lofty; his retirement from the
world was due to a real longing after holiness, and on
the whole we may recognise in him a man not unworthy
to be the sainted progenitor of the Emperors of the West,
even as Archbishop Philaret stands at the head of the
proud pedigree of the Russian Romanoffs.

Compared with the life of St. Arnulf, that of his
friend and kinsman Pippin is worldly and commonplace.
In 622, when Chlothair II. sent his son Dagobert to
reign over Austrasia, Pippin received the dignity of
mayor of the palace under the young king. By his
counsels and those of Arnulf the Eastern realm was
governed for seven years, and we are told that this
was a sort of golden age for Austrasia, in which justice
was impartially administered and prosperity prevailed.
Possibly these results were not obtained without some
sacrifice of Pippin's popularity with his brother nobles.
When Dagobert, on his father's death (in 629), removed
to Paris, his character, we are told, underwent a change.
He fell into vice and dissipation, and lost the respect
of his retainers. Pippin apparently tried to mediate
between him and them, and shared the usual fate of
mediators, earning the hatred of both parties. "The

zeal of the Austrasians surged up so vehemently against
him that they tried to make him odious in Dagobert's
eyes, that he might even be slain, but the love of justice
and the fear of God, which he had diligently embraced,
freed him from all evils." However, it seems that he,
together with other Austrasian nobles, was kept in a sort
of honourable captivity in Neustria during the rest of
the days of Dagobert (from 630 to 638), and that not
till the latter date did he return to Austrasia. Evidently
there was already an uneasy feeling on the part of the
Frankish ruler dwelling at Paris that these great
Austrasian potentates would one day give him or his
descendants a sharp struggle for the crown.

For one year after his return Pippin swayed the affairs
of the Austrasian palace, acting always in concert with
Cunibert, Bishop of Cologne, who had succeeded to the
same position of spiritual prime minister which had
formerly been held by St. Arnulf. Together they pre-
sided over the division of the treasures of the late king,
assigning one-third to his widow, Nantildis ; one-third to
his son, Clovis II., who succeeded him in Neustria, and
one-third (which with jealous care was at once conveyed
to Metz) to his other son, Sigibert III., who ruled in
Austrasia. In 640 Pippin died, greatly regretted, we
are told, by all the men of Austrasia, whose hearts he
had won by his goodness and love of justice. Possibly
during his enforced absence from the realm the Austrasian nobles had learned that the strong hand under
which they had chafed was, after all, needed for the
welfare of the State.

Some years apparently before the death of Pippin the
alliance between the two great Austrasian chiefs had

been cemented by a marriage between Adelgisel, son of
St. Arnulf, and a daughter of Pippin, who was probably
named Becga.   From this marriage sprang the second
Pippin, the great-grandfather of Charlemagne.

Adelgisel himself was mayor of the palace for a few
years before the return of his father-in-law, but he seems
to have been a somewhat insignificant person, and is
overshadowed in history by the sanctity of his father
and the success of his son.

A much more important figure is his brother-in-law,
Grimwald, son of Pippin of Landen, who three years
after his father's death succeeded, by a deed of blood
perpetrated by one of his adherents, in obtaining the
coveted mayoralty.   For thirteen years, or thereabouts,
he acted as *major domus* to the weak but devout Sigibert
III., the first of the absolutely *fainéant* kings.   Then, in
656, on the death of Sigibert, Grimwald deemed that the
time had come for ending the farce of Merovingian
royalty, shaved off the long locks of Dagobert, his dead
master's son, sent him, under the escort of the Bishop of
Poitiers, to a monastery in Ireland, and proclaimed his
own son, to whom he had given the Merovingian name
of Childebert, King of the Eastern Franks.   He was,
however, a century too soon.   The glamour which hung
round the descendants of the great Clovis had as yet
not utterly vanished, neither had the Pippins and the
Arnulfs yet done such great deeds as to give them any
title to claim the Frankish throne.   "The Franks," says
the chronicler, "being very indignant hereat, prepared
snares for Grimwald, and, taking him prisoner, carried
him for condemnation to Clovis II., King of the
Franks.   In the city of Paris he was confined in a

dungeon and bound with torturing chains; and at
length, as he was worthy of death for what he had done
to his lord, death finished him with mighty torments."

This premature clutch at royalty seems to have
damaged for a long time the fortunes of the Austrasian
house. In fact, we hear no more of the descendants of
Pippin in the male line; it is through the Arnulfings,
the posterity of Grimwald's sister, that the fortunes of
the family will one day revive.

The thirty-two years that follow (656-688) are
perhaps the dreariest in all Frankish history. The
kings, as has been said, were little better than idiots;
Austrasia was probably a prey to anarchy and dissension;
the strong and warlike races on the eastern frontier
which had been harnessed to the car of the Frankish
monarchy were rapidly breaking their bonds. The
Wends, beyond the Elbe, under a Frankish commercial
traveller named Samo (who had made himself their king,
and who had twelve wives and thirty-seven children),
had inflicted a crushing defeat on Dagobert. Dagobert's
son, Sigibert, had been defeated by Radulfus, Duke of the
Thuringians, with such a fearful slaughter of the Franks
as moved the youthful king to tears. The Alamanni were
growing restless, the Dukes of the Bavarians were
making themselves practically independent. The situation of the Frankish realm in these later years of the
seventh century was becoming like the situation of the
Mogul Empire when Clive landed in India—an old
monarchy founded on force, and long held together by
fear, but now fast falling into decomposition and ruin
through the utter loss of power in its heart.

It will be hardly necessary to waste another word on

the nominal occupants of the Frankish throne. Here, from the pages of the slightly later *Liber Historiæ Francorum*, is a picture of the reign of Clovis II., son of Dagobert, who reigned over Neustria and Burgundy from 638 to 656.

"At that time Chlodoveus (Clovis), at the instigation of the devil, broke off an arm of the blessed martyr Dionysius. At that time the kingdom of the Franks fell under many pestilential disasters. But Clovis himself was given up to every kind of filthy conversation, a fornicator and a deceiver of womankind, happy in his gluttony and drunkenness. As to his death history records nothing worth repeating, for many writers speak in condemnatory language concerning his end, but not knowing exactly how his wickedness was terminated, they talk in an uncertain way, one saying one thing and another another."

For the next quarter of a century after the death of Clovis II. the canvas is fully filled by the great figure of Ebroin, who was during many years mayor of the palace for Neustria and Burgundy, and during a short time for Austrasia also. Thus the same results, which in the next generation were secured by the ancestor of Charlemagne, seemed for a time to have been obtained by the Neustrian Ebroin. Originally raised to the dignity of mayor of the palace by something like a vote of the Frankish nobles, he used his power, when he felt himself settled in his seat, in a spirit of strenuous hostility to the aristocracy, both spiritual and temporal. That it was absolutely necessary in the interests of the kingdom that some stand should be made against the increasing pretensions of the counts and bishops there can be little doubt, but how far Ebroin acted in the interests of king and kingdom, and how far in those of his own avarice and ambition, it is now hopeless to determine. He was evidently a hard and unscrupulous man, but we have always to remember in reading the vituperative adjectives which are attached to his name that his story is written by ecclesiastics, and that he showed himself their constant opponent. Especially was he brought into collision with the astute and able Leodegarius, Bishop of Autun, who in the year 670, successfully using the name of the puppet king of Austrasia, overthrew Ebroin and his puppet, and sent the fallen *major domus* with tonsured head into retirement at Luxeuil. For three years Bishop Leodegarius ruled as practically, if not nominally, *major domus* of Burgundy; then he too fell into disgrace, became involved in an ignoble squabble with another canonised bishop, Patricius of Clermont, fled from the court, was taken captive and sent to rejoin his former rival in the monastery of Luxeuil. The assassination of Childeric, the Austrasian king (a crime which Leodegarius was afterwards accused of having prompted), led to a turn in the wheel of fortune. Leodegarius and Ebroin escaped from the monastery and succeeded in getting hold of the person of the last surviving son of Clovis II. In his name Ebroin again ruled as *major domus* in Neustria and Burgundy (674), but the alliance between him and his late fellow-prisoner was of short duration. Leodegarius was seized and blinded, and four years afterwards put to death. This Bishop of Autun was evidently a mere politician, like his far more famous successor, Talleyrand. He had less than Talleyrand's luck, and it may perhaps be admitted that, if he were not really privy to the assassination of Childeric, his punishment was somewhat harder than that usually meted out even in those days to politicians who had failed. But it is not without a slight feeling of surprise that we find this turbulent bishop transformed into a saint and martyr, and discover that Leodegarius, Bishop of Autun, is none other than the St. Leger whose name, among all those of mediæval saints, is perhaps the most often heard from the lips of Englishmen.

Restored to power, Ebroin kept his *major-domat* in Neustria and Burgundy for seven years (674-681). The same monastic biographer who pours upon his memory the names "devil," "viper," "cruel lion," and "son of damnation," confesses at the close of his career that "he had acquired such sublime glory as fell to the lot of no other Frank." About the year 679 there was civil war between the eastern and western kingdoms, and the leaders of the Austrasian army were Pippin and Martin. The former was the nobleman who is commonly called Pippin of Heristal, the grandson of St. Arnulf and Pippin of Landen; the latter was perhaps a kinsman of the Arnulfing line. Thus after more than twenty years of obscuration the great Austrasian house was once again coming to the front. Not yet, however, did victory shine upon their banners. Ebroin and his puppet king met them in battle near Laon: "An infinite crowd of people there rushed together to the fight; but the Austrasians, being conquered, turned their backs and fled. Ebroin pursued them with most cruel slaughter and laid waste the greater part of that region." Pippin escaped to Austrasia; Martin sought a refuge in Laon, but was tempted forth by Ebroin, who swore, apparently on the relics of the saints, that his life should be safe if he surrendered. Unfortunately for the suppliant the coffers, which were thought to contain the sacred dust, were really empty, and Ebroin put his outwitted victim to death with all his associates.

At last about the year 681 private vengeance ended the career of the great Neustrian Mayor. A certain nobleman named Ermenfrid, whose property Ebroin had confiscated, waited for him at his house door one Sunday morning as he was just setting out for mass, drew his sword, struck him a mortal blow on the head, and escaped to Pippin in Austrasia. The death of Ebroin meant apparently the ascendency of the eastern family. After some revolutions which it is not necessary to describe, a certain Berchar, "a man of little stature, of base education, useless in counsel," was chosen by the misguided nobles of Neustria as mayor of the palace. Against this Berchar and his king, Theodoric III., Pippin of Heristal marched with a mighty host of Austrasians. Battle was joined at a place called Textricium, now Testri, not far from St. Quentin. Berchar and his king fled from the field. The former was slain ("by his flatterers," says the chronicler), and Pippin became practically lord of the whole Frankish dominion. This event, as to the details of which we know next to nothing, but which was of immense importance for the future destinies of Europe, happened in 687. About seventy years after their first appearance in history the Arnulfings have won for themselves that high place which they will now hold in defiance of all foes till they have won a yet higher, the highest in Christendom.

CHAPTER III

THUS at last was supreme power in the Frankish kingdom concentrated in the hands of that family of statesmen
who were to hold it for two centuries.   I have been somewhat minute in tracing the history of the Neustrian
Mayoralty, but in the Austrasian kingdom it seems to
have been rather as great nobles than as Mayors of the
Palace that the Arnulfings rose to eminence.   When
Pippin won the battle of Testri he had no Austrasian
king in whose name he could fight, and he seems to
have been known simply as *Dux* or *Princeps Francorum*,
not as *Major Domus* of Austrasia.   From the scanty and
imperfect indications of the chroniclers and the bio-
graphers of saints, it would seem that before 688 all the
Eastern portion of the Frankish kingdom was (as I have
already said) in a state of disintegration, and that Pippin,
if he had been so minded, might have followed the example
of the chiefs of the Frisians, Thuringians, and Bavarians,
by setting up for himself as a virtually independent
Duke of Austrasia.   What constitutes the peculiar world-
historical importance of this Arnulfing is that he was
not satisfied with this easy solution of the problem

before him, but using his great position in Austrasia as
a lever made himself supreme also in Neustria and
Burgundy, and then as *major domus* of a legitimate
though utterly effete Merovingian king, compelled the
unruly chiefs on the Eastern frontier to return to their
old allegiance, and thus became in fact the second
founder of the Frankish monarchy. That monarchy
seems indeed to us who labour through its barbarous
annals about as miserable a political machine as the
Aryan nations have ever invented ; but, however bad it
may have been, it was probably the best that could then
be contrived for the united government of the countries
between the Bay of Biscay and the mountains of
Bohemia; and for the time it was all important for
Europe that these countries should still form part of
one state.

For some years Pippin ruled the Western realm by
means of a loyal adherent, Nordbert, to whom however he did not concede the fateful title of mayor.
About fourteen years after the battle of Testri we find
his son Grimwald recognised as *major domus* for
Neustria and probably his eldest son Drogo held the
same office in Burgundy. Meanwhile Pippin, returning
to his own Austrasian lands, was warring down the
German pretenders to independence. The Frisian
Ratbod was defeated in a great battle, compelled to
cede West Friesland to the Franks, and to acknowledge
in fact as well as in name the supremacy of the Merovingian *fainéant*. Though himself a heathen, Ratbod
was fain to give his daughter—who was no doubt converted to Christianity—in marriage to Pippin's son
Grimwald ; and the Anglo-Saxon preacher Willibrord

had a clear course given him for his missionary operations among the Frisians. So too the Alamanni and the Bavarians appear to have been brought back into subjection by Pippin, though we hear less of his operations on the Danube than by the mouths of the Rhine.

For twenty-seven years this strong and statesman-like man ruled with absolute sway the kingdom of the Franks, and then in his old age, by one act of supreme folly, went near to ruining the whole achievement of a lifetime. As it was said of old, "Let no man be called happy," so may we add, "Let no man be called wise, till his death." He had married in early life a lady named Plectrudis, nobly born and with a reputation for prudence and ability, by whom he had two sons, Drogo and Grimwald. Drogo had died in 708, leaving two sons who were now growing up to manhood. Grimwald, who had married, as before said, a Frisian princess, had no son by her, but was the father of an illegitimate son, a little child named Theudwald.

As for Pippin himself, like many other members of his house, though descended from the sainted Arnulf, and generally on very good terms with the Church, he seems to have been guilty of great laxity in his matrimonial relations. Assuredly the Arnulfings did not plunge into those excesses of profligacy which destroyed the vigour of the Merovingian line, yet there was a tendency in many of them to take a polygamous view of marriage, more suited to an Arabian Caliph than to a Christian nobleman. Thus we find that Pippin had another wife named Alphaida, who, though the relationship was an interlude in his married life with Plectrudis, is yet treated by the chroniclers not as a concubine, but as a lawfully wedded wife. To a son born of this marriage Pippin had given the name of Charles. According to an old Saga, when the child was born, the messenger came into the presence of the great mayor of the palace and, dismayed at seeing him sitting with Plectrudis by his side, shouted out "Long live the king. It is a Carl," the old German word for a man. "And a very good name, too," said Pippin. "Let him be called Carl." This Charles, son of Alphaida, was in the year 714 a strong and vigorous man of between twenty and thirty, already married and father of an eight-year-old son.

Now, when the aged Pippin was lying on that which was to prove his death-bed (at the villa of Jovius, near Liège), his son Grimwald, a man "pitiful, moderate, and just," who was his universally recognised heir, was on his way to visit him and receive his last commands, when for some unknown reason he was assassinated in a church at Liège by a heathen named Rangar. This was a cruel blow for the dying chieftain, but as far as the future of his house was concerned not an irreparable one. His obvious policy was to declare that Charles, the son of Alphaida, was to be his heir in room of the murdered Grimwald. Instead of this, influenced no doubt by his wife's hatred of her step-son, he committed the inconceivable folly of passing over Charles, and naming, not even one of Drogo's adolescent sons, but the childish Theudwald, son of Grimwald, his heir, and designating him for the mayoralty under the regency of Plectrudis. This was an absolutely preposterous arrangement and one foredoomed to failure. The Merovingian king, *fainéant* of course, but a lad of fifteen years old, was to have a little child of eight thrust upon him as adviser, factotum, supreme prime minister, and the nominal advice of the baby was to be given through the lips of his grandmother, a harsh and domineering old woman. Such a scheme of administering the affairs of a great kingdom crumbled, as it was sure to crumble, at the first contact with actual fact.

"Plectrudis," we are told by the chronicler, "with her grandsons and the king governed all things by her discreet rule." One of the early acts of this discreet rule was to shut up her step-son Charles in prison. But deliverance for the Arnulfing house came from an unexpected quarter. The nobles of Neustria, indignant probably at being calmly transferred to the dominion of a beldame and a child, proclaimed one of their own class, a certain Raginfrid, *major domus* and supported his pretensions with an army. Neustria and Austrasia met in battle at the Cotian Forest, not far from Compiègne, and Neustria won a decided victory, the baby-mayor, who had been brought into the field at the head of the Austrasian *leudes*, being with difficulty carried off by his partisans. Raginfrid pressed on and formed an alliance with old Ratbod, the Frisian, and apparently with the Saxons also. Plectrudis, shut up in Cologne, saw her power slipping from her and the Austrasian state threatened with ruin. The disorganisation which everywhere prevailed had at least this advantage, that in the confusion Charles escaped from his prison (715). He gathered round him some of his father's adherents: he fought Raginfrid, his puppet king, and the Frisians: fought them at first unsuccessfully, for they pushed on to Cologne where Plectrudis was fain to purchase peace for herself and her grandsons by the surrender of a

large part of the royal hoard. After this she and
Theudwald disappear from history. Charles, whose
powers of recovery the Neustrians appear to have
under-rated, follows them westwards in 716 and wins
a great victory over them at Amblève and another next
year at Vincy. Raginfrid sees no prospect of defending
his puppet king (to whom Charles has set up a rival)
except by seeking the help of Eudo, the great Duke of
Aquitaine, who as a practically independent sovereign,
is ruling all the region south of the Loire. Eudo
and Raginfrid join forces and advance as far as Soissons
(719) : then for some unexplained cause Eudo turns
back and leaves Raginfrid to face the enemy alone.
Charles wins a third great victory, and now Raginfrid's
resistance is practically at an end. He submits on certain
conditions to Charles, who becomes (in 720) unquestioned
major domus of all the three kingdoms, while Raginfrid
subsides eventually into some such position as Count of
Angers, where he prolongs his resistance till 724.

The Arnulfing hero who out of such a chaos of opposing
forces succeeded in evoking that order and stable government which the Frankish State so greatly needed,
received, apparently from his contemporaries, the name
of Martel or the Hammer. This epithet, which has
been sometimes connected with his great victory over
the Saracens, seems to be more truly derived from his
exploits in the earlier part of his career, destroying as
he did with his smashing blows, the petty tyrannies
which had grown up in the anarchy that followed the
death of his father.

It is worthy of note that Charles, unlike his father,
did not delegate his mayoralty in Neustria and Bur-

gundy to any one, even a son, and that he styled himself
major domus for Austrasia as well as for the other
kingdoms, a title which for some reason seems not to
have been claimed by his father. It is also noteworthy
that he finally got the needed Merovingian *fainéant* into
his possession by a compromise with Eudo of Aquitaine
who had carried him off from the unfought battlefield of
Soissons. There are many indications that both Eudo
and Charles felt the necessity of sparing one another's
strength and not pushing any dispute between them to
extremities, in view of the far more tremendous danger
which threatened them and all Christendom from the
turbaned followers of the Prophet who were now
beginning to swarm over the passes of the Pyrenees.

It was in 711, three years before Pippin's death, that
the Visigothic monarchy of Spain fell before the Moslem
invader. In 716 the Moors seem to have first entered
Gaul in detached squadrons. In 720, the year after the
campaign of Soissons, they invaded Gaul in force, took
Narbonne and established themselves in the old Visigothic province of Septimania, from which they were
not finally dislodged for nearly forty years. They be-
seiged Toulouse with many great engines of war, and their
retreat from this place, compelled by the appearance of
Duke Eudo with an army, may be noted as the first sign
of ebb in the tide of Moslem conquest in Western
Europe.

It was, however, twelve years before the Mussulman's
hope of adding Gaul to the Empire of the Caliph
received its death-stroke. In 725 they penetrated as
far as Autun, in the very heart of Burgundy, demolished
the city and carried off the treasures of the Church to

Spain. The vigilance of Eudo of Aquitaine seems to have relaxed, and he was now no longer, as in 720, the great champion of Gaulish Christendom against the invader. On the contrary he entered into friendly relations with at least one Mussulman warrior, bestowing his daughter Lampegia on Munuza, a Berber chieftain, who seems to have been striving to establish a Moorish kingdom in Spain independent of the Caliphs. It was perhaps owing to this new combination that Eudo broke through the treaty which he had made with Charles in 720. There were thus two princes, a Christian and a Moor, Eudo and Munuza, each rebelling against the state to which they nominally owed allegiance. However, neither attempt at independence was destined to succeed : Charles twice crossed the Loire in the year 731, defeated Eudo in battle, apparently near the city of Bourges, and returned home with great booty, having effectually checked the separatist designs of the Aquitanian chief. About the same time apparently, Abderrahman, the legitimate representative of the Caliph of Damascus, overthrew the Berber chief Munuza and hunted him into the Pyrenees, where he was overtaken while resting by a fountain. Munuza fell pierced with many wounds, and his bride, Eudo's daughter, was sent to end her days in the Caliph's harem.

Thus then were all the side issues disposed of, and the ground was cleared for the great, the real issue between the Mohammedan power reaching from Damascus to the Pyrenees, and the Christian power which was embodied in the Frankish monarchy, but whose central point was now to be found in the home of the great *major domus* by the Rhine. Abderrahman, a brave and capable warrior, the chief who alone had gotten glory out of the great expedition of 720, when he led the beaten host back from Toulouse, prepared a great armament for the conquest of Gaul, and in the spring of 732 started from Pampelona on an expedition, as full of meaning for the future history of the human race as was that armament of Xerxes which found its doom at Salamis. The overflowing flood of the Islamites soon spread beyond the limits of Gascony. In Perigord Eudo met them, Eudo now cured of all desire to coalesce with the Mussulman and probably longing to revenge Lampegia's wrongs on her captor, Abderrahman. He was, however, utterly defeated by the banks of the river Dronne and lost the greater part of his army. The Moorish host pushed on towards the Loire; and now, had the Frankish monarchy been in the same condition as seventeen years before, with Neustria and Austrasia divided against one another, and the Austrasian *major-domat* put in commission between an old woman and a child, the Moorish invasion must to all appearance have carried everything before it. But when Abderrahman had reached Poitiers, and burnt the Church of St. Hilary, the tide of his success was stayed. Eudo, a fugitive and despairing, had sought the help of his late adversary Charles, and the great *major domus* with a host of stout-hearted Austrasians was posted between the rivers Clain and Vienne, blocking the old Roman road from Poitiers to Tours. For seven days the armies stood watching one another, while Abderrahman was probably trying to turn the Frankish position. Then at last, on a certain Saturday in October, finding that only the sword could open up the road, he sent the masses of his turbaned followers against the Frankish position. In vain they dashed against that moveless barrier. "The Northern nations," says the Spanish chronicler Isidore, "stood immovable as a wall, or as if frozen to their places by the rigorous breath of winter, but hewing down the Arabs with their swords. But when the Austrasian people by the might of their massive limbs, and with iron hands striking straight from the chest their strenuous blows, had laid multitudes of the enemy low, at last they found the king [Abderrahman], and robbed him of life. Then night disparted the combatants, the Franks brandishing their swords on high in scorn of the enemy. Next day, rising at earliest dawn and seeing the innumerable tents of the Arabs all ranged in order before them, the Europeans prepared for fight, deeming that within those tents were the phalanxes of the enemy; but sending forth their scouts they found that the hosts of the Ishmaelites had fled away silently under cover of the night, seeking their own country. Fearing, however, a feigned flight, and a sudden return by hidden ways, they circled round and round with amazed caution and thus the invaders escaped, but the Europeans after dividing the spoils and the captives in orderly manner among themselves returned with gladness to their homes."

So, in uncouth and not always intelligible words, does the Spanish ecclesiastic tell the story of that great day, which decided that not the Koran but the Gospel was to be the guide of the conscience of Europe. To Charles Martel and his stalwart Austrasians struggling through that terrible Saturday in October, is it due that the muezzin is not at noon to-day calling the faithful to prayer from some high minaret by the Seine. It was said that the Franks on this day slew 375,000 Saracens, losing only 1500 of their own men. The numbers are evidently but a wild and baseless guess, but the strange thing is that they could be thus reported by a sober and cautious historian, and one not of the Frankish nation (Paulus Diaconus), writing barely sixty years after the date of the famous victory.

The Moslem invaders were weakened, but not absolutely crushed by this great encounter. They still kept their hold on the sea-coast of Languedoc, the region which having been for three centuries in the possession of the Visigoths was still known as Gothia. In 737 they crossed the Rhone, and forming a league with a certain Maurontus (who was perhaps Duke of Provence), they obtained possession of the strongly fortified city of Avignon. Charles, whose normal occupation was warfare with the Frisians and Saxons, was recalled from the Rhine-lands in order to do battle with the Islamite in the valley of the Rhone. Avignon was recaptured and Charles marched on to Narbonne, the citadel of the Saracen power in Gaul. But though he defeated the Mussulmans in a great battle by the sea-coast, he failed to take Narbonne. Nismes and several other towns in Languedoc were recovered from the misbelievers; their walls were demolished, and the great amphitheatre of Nismes was somehow dismantled so as to prevent its again affording cover to the enemy, but Narbonne was still Islamite at the death of Charles.

In the same year in which this encounter took place, died Theodoric IV., the *fainéant* Merovingian who for

seventeen years had been the figure-head at the prow of
the vessel of the State. Charles did not covet the mere
name of royalty, nor was he disposed to imitate the
disastrous example of his great-uncle Grimwald; but,
as the needful Childeric or Chilperic was not at the
time forthcoming, he dispensed with the luxury of a
roi fainéant, and for the remaining four years of his life
reigned alone, mayor of a palace in which no king was
to be found.

The career of Charles Martel was now drawing to a
close. He was again, in 738, recalled from his operations against the Saxons, by tidings of the invasion of
Provence by the Saracens in league with the turbulent
Maurontus. For that year the danger was averted by
the help of the Lombard king Liutprand, the friend
and brother-in-law of Charles. Next year Charles
himself invaded Provence with a large army, brought
the whole of that beautiful land into real instead of
nominal subjection to the Frankish State, and broke the
power of Maurontus, who, a hunted fugitive, escaped
with difficulty over the craggy cliffs of the Riviera,
which are now linked together by the great highway of
the Cornice.

But, this exploit performed, Charles began to sicken.
He was still little more than fifty years of age, but his
incessant wars, his rapid marches and counter-marches
between the German Ocean and the Pyrenees had worn
out his strenuous frame. The hammer would strike
no more blows for the welding together of the Frankish
State. The piteous appeals of Pope Gregory III., who
implored his assistance against the Lombard assailants
of Rome, fell on unwilling ears. Charles had some-

thing else now to do than to cross the Alps and wage
war on his friend and kinsman Liutprand, who had
been his helper against the Islamites, and to whom he
had sent his son Pippin to be adopted as his *filius per
arma*, a ceremony similar to the bestowal of knighthood
in a later day.   In 740 the extraordinary fact is recorded,
that no warlike expedition was undertaken by the
Franks.   The great *major domus* seems to have been
chiefly occupied in arranging for the partition of his
territories—they were now without hesitation called his
—among his three sons.   On the 22nd of October 741
he died at his villa of Quierzy on the Oise, and was buried
in that great abbey of St. Denis, which was to receive
the corpses of so many sovereigns of his own and other
races.

Though the descendant of the sainted Arnulf, though
the champion of Christendom against the Saracens, and
the strong protector of the "apostles" who, relying on
the sharpness of the Frankish battle-axe, went forth to
convert the heathen Frisians and Saxons, Charles Martel
was looked upon with no favour by the ecclesiastics of
his time.   By the grants of *fainéant* kings and honourable women, the possessions of the Church in Gaul had
grown so enormously as to weaken the resources of the
kingdom, and Charles found himself, or believed himself,
compelled to lay his hand upon some of all this accumulated wealth for the defence of Gaul and Christendom.   He did it in the most dangerous way for the
Church, not by revoking grants or imposing taxes on
ecclesiastical property, but by conferring prelacies and
abbacies on trusty friends and followers of his own, men
who were without any pretensions to the spiritual

character, but upon whom he might rely to use the Church's wealth on the right side. Thus, we find already emerging the question which three or four centuries later, in the days of Hildebrand and the Franconian Emperors, took peace from the earth. It is easy to see how such a manner of disposing of ecclesiastical property would rouse the opposition of all that was highest as well as of all that was lowest in the Gaulish Church, of genuine zeal for holiness as well as of mere greed and worldly ambition. Thus it came to pass, that while the rest of the Arnulfing line were venerated as friends and patrons of the Church, Charles Martel fared more hardly at her hands, and the superstition of the times—

> " Doomed him to the Zealot's ready hell,
> Which " pleads the Church's claims " so eloquently well."

In the next century a libellous vision was forged by a famous archbishop, according to which a prelate saw Charles Martel suffering the torments of hell, and, on asking the cause, was told that it was his allotted penalty for seizing on the domains of the Church. The dreaming prelate, on awaking, went, so it was said, to the abbey of St. Denis and opened Charles's tomb, but found no corpse therein, only a blackened shell, out of which a winged dragon rushed and flew rapidly away.

CHAPTER IV

THE unity of the Frankish State, so dearly purchased by the heroic labours of Charles Martel, was as usual placed in jeopardy by the dying ruler's arrangements for the succession to that which was now openly spoken of as his "principatus."

He left two sons, Carloman and Pippin, by his first wife Hrotrudis, and one, Grifo, by a Bavarian princess named Swanahild, whom he had married after an invasion of her country, and whose sister was the wife of the Lombard king Liutprand.

This was the manner in which Charles Martel divided his dominions among his sons. To the eldest, Carloman, he gave the greater part of Austrasia, Alamannia, and Thuringia; to Pippin, the younger, Neustria, Burgundy and Provence. Apparently both Aquitaine in the south-west, and Bavaria in the south-east were too nearly independent to be thus disposed of by a ruler who, after all, was still in theory only the chief adviser of a Merovingian king, though that king's royalty was for the present in abeyance.

To Grifo, whose turbulent attempts at insurrection,

aided by his mother Swanahild, had troubled the last years of Charles, was assigned a small central state carved out of all the three realms, Austrasia, Neustria, and Burgundy, at their point of meeting. "As to this third portion," says the chronicler, "which the dying prince had assigned to the young man Grifo, the Franks were sorely displeased that by the advice of a wicked woman they should be cut up and separated from the lawful heirs. Taking counsel together and joining with them the princes Carloman and Pippin, they collected an army for the capture of Grifo, who, hearing of their intent, took to flight, together with his mother Swanahild and all who were willing to follow him, and all shut themselves up in Lugdunum Clavatum (Laon). But Grifo, seeing that he could not possibly escape, surrendered himself to the keeping of his brothers. Carloman receiving the captive sent him to be kept in safe custody at the New Castle (Neuf Château in the Ardennes) : and they placed Swanahild in the monastery of Cala (Chelles near Paris)."

We shall rapidly pass in review the events which led to the concentration of the whole power of the State in the hands of Pippin alone, but first we must notice that for some unexplained reason, possibly in order to give them a better title to the obedience of Aquitaine and Bavaria, the princely brothers decided to bring the kingless period to an end. In 743 Childeric III. was placed on the throne. He was probably about twenty years of age, but the date of his birth, and even his place in the royal pedigree are doubtful. Of his character, of course, we know nothing. He is but the shadow of a shadow, this last Merovingian king.

Very different from shadows were the two Arnulfing brothers, as they warred with Hunald, Duke of Aquitaine (son of their father's old troubler Eudo), with Odilo, Duke of Bavaria, with the heathen Saxons, with the restless and disloyal Alamanni. Of the two brothers, Pippin seems to have been somewhat the gentler. It was Carloman the strong and stern warrior, who, infuriated by the faithlessness of the Alamanni, entered their territory, called a muster of their warriors at Cannstadt (near Stuttgart), and then surrounding them by his Franks, disarmed them, and slew many of their leaders. The accounts of this assembly at Cannstadt are dark and perplexing, but on comparing them it certainly seems probable that there was great severity on the part of Carloman, probably treachery and possibly widespread slaughter.

Was it remorse for this bloody deed which changed the character and career of Carloman? It is not expressly so said by any of the chroniclers, yet the statement seems a probable inference from their meagre notices. For it was in the same year (746) in which the strange transaction with the Alamanni had taken place at Cannstadt that Carloman began to talk to his brother Pippin concerning his desire to relinquish the world and devote himself to the service of Almighty God : "Therefore both the brothers made their preparations, Carloman that he might go to the threshold of the apostles Peter and Paul, and Pippin that his brother might make the journey with all honour and splendid gifts."

Carloman's decision to embrace the monastic life was not an unexampled sacrifice for a ruler in that day.

Sixty years before, Ceadwalla, King of the West Saxons, and twenty years before, his royal kinsman Ine had left their palaces and come to live and die as tonsured monks in Rome.   Two years before Carloman's abdication, Hunald of Aquitaine, and three years after it, Ratchis the Lombard took the same step.   Still, the splendid position which Carloman abandoned, and the lowliness of his demeanour after his abdication, touched and awed the hearts of his contemporaries.

In 747 Carloman formally renounced his share of power, and went with a long train of nobles and with costly presents in his hand to Rome, "to the threshold of the apostle Peter."   There he submitted to the tonsure and received the clerical habit from Pope Zacharias. After a time, by the pope's advice, he withdrew to the mountain solitude of Soracte, twenty-eight miles from Rome, where he erected a monastery in honour of St. Sylvester.   This saint was the Bishop of Rome who, according to an ecclesiastical fable which was just at this time obtaining wide currency, received from the Emperor Constantine the celebrated "Donation" of Rome and the larger part of Italy.   The fable also related that Sylvester had previously sought a refuge in Mount Soracte from the persecution ordained by Constantine while still a Pagan, and had afterwards cured that emperor of leprosy by directing him to a pool on the mountain in which he was to perform a threefold immersion. It need hardly be said that all this is utterly valueless as history, but as it was in that uncritical age accepted as unquestioned truth, the fact that the enthusiast Carloman sought the solitudes of Soracte for the place of his retirement and there dedicated his monastery to St.

Sylvester is important as showing what was passing in
the minds of men, and especially of devout Frankish
princes in that age.   Later on, he left his mountain
home in Soracte and sought the far-famed monastery
of St. Benedict on Monte Cassino.   Tradition said that
he fled thither by night, with one faithful squire,
his companion from infancy, and with no sign of his
once high dignity.   Knocking at the door of the convent he desired speech with the abbot, and when that
dignitary appeared, threw himself on the ground before
him, confessing that he was a murderer and praying to
be allowed to expiate his crime by repentance in the
monastery.   The abbot, seeing that he was a foreigner
asked him of his race and country.   "I am a Frank,"
said Carloman, "and for my crime I have left my native
land of Francia.   I heed not exile if only I may not fail
of the heavenly fatherland."   He was received into the
cell of the novices with his companion and was subjected to severe discipline, as became a man of barbarous race and unknown name, for the abbot was
mindful of the apostolic precept, "Try the spirits
whether they are of God."   To all these hardships and
humiliations Carloman submitted with exemplary
patience.   It chanced at last that it fell to his lot as
a novice to take a week's turn in the kitchen of the
convent.   He did his work zealously but made many
blunders, for which the head cook, heated with wine,
rewarded him with a slap on the face.   Meekly the
princely scullion replied, "Is that how you ought to
serve the brethren?   May God pardon you, my brother,
and Carloman too."   The last words were perhaps uttered
under his breath, for he had not yet revealed his name

to anyone. A second and a third time this incident was repeated, and on the last occasion the cook's blows were cruel and brutal. His faithful squire could then bear the sight no longer. He snatched up the pestle with which the bread was being pounded for the brethren's soup, and struck the head cook with all his might, saying, "Neither may God spare thee, vile slave, nor may Carloman forgive thee." Then followed uproar, indignation at the foreigner's presumption, arrest, imprisonment. Next day the squire was set in the midst of the assembled monks and asked why he had dared to stretch forth his hand against a serving brother. "Because," he answered, "I was indignant at seeing a slave, the meanest of mankind, not only flout and jeer, but actually strike a man, the best and noblest of all that I have ever met with on the earth." The angry monks demanded who was this man whom he, a foreigner, dared to rank before all others, not even excepting the abbot himself. Thus was the truth forced out of him, since it was the will of God that it should no longer be concealed. "That man is Carloman, formerly ruler of the Franks, who, for the love of Christ hath left his kingdom and the glory of the world : who from such high estate has so humbled himself as to be subject not only to the insults but even to the blows of the vilest of men." Then the monks rose from their seats in terror and prostrated themselves at the feet of Carloman, imploring his forgiveness for aught that they might have done to him in ignorance of his rank. Vainly did he in turn grovel on the earth before them and try to assure them that his comrade had lied and that he was not Carloman. He was recognised by all, held in the highest reverence, and as we shall afterwards see, was selected by the abbot for an important mission.

On the abdication of Carloman, Grifo was liberated by Pippin from his imprisonment which had lasted six years, received by him in his palace with every mark of honour and affection, and invested with several countships and large revenues. This was not enough, however, for Grifo, who probably aspired to an equal share of his father's late dominions. He allied himself with the Saxons and shared their defeat in battle (748); he sought refuge in Bavaria, and for a time made himself duke of that country (749); expelled from thence by Pippin he betook himself first to Aquitaine and then to the King of the Lombards, but was met at Maurienne by Count Theodowin, who was guarding the passes of the Alps in the Frankish interest. A skirmish followed, in which many Frankish nobles fell, Grifo himself and Theodowin among them (753). There was no further obstacle raised by any member of the Arnulfing family to the sole domination of Pippin.

Fateful for all the after-history of Europe were the middle years of the eighth century, upon which we have now entered. The time had at last come when Pippin, virtual sovereign of Gaul and Western Germany, could venture to take the step which had proved fatal to his kinsman Grimwald, and to bring names and facts into accord by proclaiming himself King of the Franks. But in taking this step it behoved him to be sure of two things, the consent of the nation and the sanction of the Church. By the advice and with the consent of all the Franks, expressed no doubt by some assembly of the chief men of the nation, two great ecclesiastics, Fulrad,

Abbot of St. Denis representing Neustria, and Burchard, Bishop of Würzburg representing Austrasia, were sent to Rome to ask the opinion of the pope on the great problem. It will be well to state their commission in the words of a contemporary chronicler :

"In the year 750 [it should be 751] from the incarnation of our Lord, Pippin sends ambassadors to Rome to Zacharias the Pope to ask concerning the Kings of the Franks who were of the royal race and were called kings, but had no power in the kingdom except only that grants and charters were drawn up in their names, but they had absolutely no royal power; but what the *major domus* of the Franks willed, that they did. But on the [first] day of March in the *Campus* [*Martis*] according to ancient custom gifts were offered to those kings by the people, and the king himself sat on the royal throne with the army standing round him and the *major domus* close by, and on that day he gave forth as his orders whatever had been decreed by the Franks, but on every other day thenceforward he sat quietly at home. Pope Zacharias thereupon answered their question according to his apostolic authority, that it seemed better and more expedient to him that *he* should be called and be king who had power in the kingdom rather than he who was falsely called king. Therefore the aforesaid pope commanded the king and people of the Franks that Pippin who exercised the royal power should be called king and be placed on the royal seat; which was accordingly done by the anointing of the holy archbishop Boniface in the city of Soissons. Pippin is called king, and Childeric who falsely bore that title receives the tonsure and is sent into a monastery."

So at length was the great change accomplished towards which Frankish history had been tending for more than a century. What happened was undoubtedly a revolution, though of a peaceful kind. The papal sanction, the archiepiscopal unction might impress the minds of the multitude; this new Christian consecration might partly compensate for the missing glamour of a descent from gods and heroes which had surrounded the dynasty of the Merovings; but in strict right, of course, the Bishop of Rome had no title to command the change, no power to absolve the Salian and Ripuarian Franks from their plighted faith to the descendants of Clovis. It was well thought of to put the scene of the consecration of the new dynasty at Soissons, that place so memorable in the history of the older race. It was also important, if the pope himself could not be induced to cross the Alps to perform the ceremony of anointing, to have it performed by Boniface the Apostle of the Germans, and the most conspicuous ecclesiastical figure in Europe.

We may pause for a moment to notice the remarkable share taken by this man and others of our fellow-countrymen in bringing about the conversion of large portions of the German nation to Christianity, and indirectly in founding the Teutonic "Holy Roman Empire" of the Middle Ages. Scarcely had the Anglo-Saxon peoples been won over to the Christian Church, when they began with missionary zeal to preach the faith among their still heathen kinsmen on the Continent. The mission of St. Augustine to Britain took place in the year 596. In 634 was born the Northumbrian Wilfrid, and in 658 his countryman Willibrord, both of

whom laboured with zeal and success for the conversion
of the heathens of Friesland. A generation later the
young Devonian Winifried, born at Crediton, appeared
on the banks of the Lower Rhine, to profit by the experience of the aged Willibrord and to catch his falling
mantle. Three times he visited Rome to confer with those
great popes, the second and the third Gregory, and to
receive their orders for the conversion of fresh tribes in
Germany, or for the consolidation of spiritual conquests
already achieved. On one of these visits, probably, he
received that name of Boniface by which he is best
known in history, together with a sort of roving commission as archbishop, and authority to act as legate in
the churches of Germany. Armed with this power he
set up bishoprics in Bavaria, revived the dying Christianity of Thuringia, and chastised heretics in Gaul.
Wherever the armies of Charles Martel marched, in
Friesland, in Saxony, in Hesse, Archbishop Boniface
followed, smashing idols, felling sacred oaks, and baptiz-
ing half-unwilling converts. Towards the end of his
life his roving commission was changed into the more
stationary office of Archbishop of Mainz, and he sometimes retired for repose to the great monastery of Fulda,
which he had founded in the Hessian land near the
source of the Weser. But the old war-horse was still
stirred by the sound of the trumpet. Three years after
his consecration of Pippin, Boniface went forth on a last
expedition for the conversion of the Frisians. When he
reached Dockum (in the north of the present province of
Friesland) he found there, instead of the expected cate-
chumens, a multitude of the heathens, zealous for the
honour of their idols which Boniface had so often

destroyed, and eager for the spoil of the ecclesiastical invader. From their hands he received the crown of martyrdom for which he longed.

The career of Boniface is of especial importance, because of his absolute devotion to the see of Rome. It was observed that the recently converted nations, as is so often the case with new converts, surpassed their older brethren in the fervour of their faith. While the bishops of Gaul were lukewarm, sometimes almost insubordinate, the Anglo-Saxon bishops were the devoted adherents of the papacy. Boniface especially professed the most unbounded reverence for the chair of St. Peter, and took with alacrity an oath of implicit obedience, substantially the same which was exacted from the "suburbicarian" bishops of the sees in the immediate neighbourhood of Rome. This was the spirit in which the infant churches were trained, and this no doubt was the tenour of the advice which the zealous Archbishop of Mainz gave to the new King of the Franks on the day of his coronation.

A traveller through the pleasant valleys of Devonshire when he comes to the little town, scarcely more than a village, of Crediton between its two overhanging hills, may reflect with interest that he beholds the birthplace of the man who, more than any other, brought about the entrance of the German nation into the family of Christian Europe.

The coronation of Pippin took place probably about November 751. In four months from that time Pope Zacharias died, doubtless without any presentiment of the abiding importance of the event in which by his answer to the Frankish messengers he had borne a part,

but which is not even mentioned by his biographer in
the *Liber Pontificalis*. After a short interval, an ecclesiastic of Roman parentage, who figures in the annals of
the papacy as Stephen II., was raised to the papal see,
His pontificate was short; it lasted but five years, but
they were years full of import for the destinies of
Europe.

In order to concentrate our attention on the transformation of the Arnulfing mayors of the palace into
Frankish kings, I have hitherto said as little as possible
about the affairs of Italy, but this silence can be kept
no longer, now that a Roman pope is about to cross
the Alps and ask for Frankish aid to enable him to smite
down his foes.

The Lombards had invaded Italy in the year 568,
and for nearly two centuries from that time there had
been waged a kind of triangular contest which, to com-
pare great things with small, was like the litigation
which might go on in an English parish between an
absentee landlord, a big Nonconformist farmer, and a
cultured but acquisitive parson.

The Emperor was the great absentee. Though still
always spoken of as Emperor of Rome, he had been in
fact for some centuries an absolutely Oriental Sovereign.
Since the deposition of Romulus Augustulus in 476, no
Roman Emperor had touched the soil of Italy save for one
brief and most unwelcome visit paid by Constans II. in
663. The Imperial dominion in the peninsula was by
this time limited to the Venetian islands, two provinces
on the Adriatic coast called the Exarchate of Ravenna
and the Pentapolis, the city of Hydruntum (Otranto),
the province of Bruttii at the very end of the pen-

insula, Paestum, Naples and the duchy of Rome, which included the city of Rome, the present province of Latium and a little bit of Etruria. This scattered and fragmentary dominion, which as will be seen was almost entirely confined to the sea-coast, and embraced only a part of that, was ruled by an imperial lieutenant who bore the title of Exarch, and whose seat of government was the strong, almost impregnable city of Ravenna.

Far the largest part of Italy, including all the fertile valley of the Po, all the central chain of the Apennines and the valleys leading from them, the greater part of Tuscany and almost the whole of Apulia, was in the possession of the rough and masterful Lombards, who had been fierce savages when they entered Italy, but who had lost most of their savagery and some of their warlike vigour by long residence in the delightful land and by contact with the vestiges of Roman civilisation. Arians for the most part, and even with some heathens among them at the time of their first invasion, they had now embraced the Catholic faith, were generous benefactors of the Church, and desired to be considered her dutiful sons. But still the remembrance of their old heresies continued, and whenever the political interests of the King of the Lombards clashed with those of the Pope of Rome—and they did clash as often and as irreconcilably as do those of pope and king at the present day—the old epithets " unspeakable," " sacrilegious," " diabolical," flowed from the pens of the scribes in the papal chancery as freely as they had flowed when the Lombards were yet idolaters.

As for the pope, how describe in few words his

anomalous and fast-changing position? Undoubted
Patriarch of the Western Church, he nevertheless had
many a struggle with the Patriarch of Constantinople
as to his claim to rule the Church Universal. The
missionaries whom he had sent forth to convert the
Teutonic tribes of England and Germany were, as has
been said, zealous asserters of his spiritual pre-eminence,
and, like the Jesuits of the sixteenth and seven-
teenth centuries, the great champions of the rights of
Rome. Herein also they were vigorously supported by
the monks who had spread widely over all Christian
lands, and who at this time were almost without exception followers of the rule of the Italian saint, Benedict.
Some of the bishops, however, especially some of the
Gaulish bishops, were, as has been said, by no means
equally prompt in their obedience to the papal see. The
pope's relation to the distant emperor at Constantinople
during these centuries of transition is one of the hardest
things to describe with accuracy. A subject, and yet in a
certain sense a rival, often severely snubbed by the
emperor's representative at Rome, almost adored on one
or two occasions when he set foot in Constantinople;
elected by the clergy and people of Old Rome, yet for
many generations not venturing to assume the title of
pope till he received the imperial confirmation from
New Rome; a mere ecclesiastic without as yet any pretension to temporal sovereignty, and yet under the
stress of circumstances ordering campaigns against the
Lombards, installing dukes and displacing tribunes—
such in the time of Gregory the Great and for more than
a century afterwards had been the anomalous relation
of the *beatissimus Papa* or *sanctissimus Pontifex*, to his

serenissimus Dominus, Christianissimus principum, the man
who at Constantinople wore the diadem of Diocletian.
The relation was strained and difficult, and one would
have said that it could not long endure; and yet (as
anomalies, especially in the relations of Church and
State, are apt to do), it lasted long, for at least six
generations of mankind. During this time the popes
had certainly often to complain of harsh and overbearing
treatment on the part of their imperial masters. One
pope was dragged from the altar to a dungeon; another
was banished to the Crimea, and died in that remote
place of exile; the life of another was conspired against
by murderers in the pay of the emperor's Italian representative, and these were only the more striking passages
in a long history of estrangement and mutual suspicion.
Through all, the hold of the pope on the affections of the
Roman people was steadily increasing, since he was
looked upon as the representative of Roman nationality
and Roman orthodoxy against the often schismatical
Greek and the always domineering Lombard.

Of late—that is to say, during the greater part of
the mayoralty of Charles Martel—the antagonism
between pope and emperor had been increased by the
dispute about the worship of images. In 726 Leo III.,
the great Isaurian emperor who had successfully repelled
the Saracens from the walls of Constantinople, put forth
his edicts for the destruction of the sacred images
throughout the empire. These decrees, which roused
some of the Greeks to actual insurrection, were met by
sullen disobedience on the part of the Italians. The
authority of the Exarch of Ravenna was set at naught;
the local government was vested in dukes chosen by the

enraged image-worshippers; it seemed as though the empire would utterly lose even the vestiges of its dominion in Italy. But at this crisis the pope (Gregory II.), though he had been in strong opposition to the emperor, and had sharply denounced his iconoclastic edicts, restrained the Italians from actual revolt and from the election of a counter-emperor, "hoping for the conversion of the sovereign." It is difficult to say how the matter ended. Apparently the decrees were not enforced in Italy, nor did the movement of insurrection gather head. The exarch still ruled in Ravenna; the pope still considered himself the subject of the eastern emperor; but there was no cordiality between them, and more and more the popes looked across the Alps to the new Austrasian potentate, rather than to the old Augustus by the Bosphorus, for defence, patronage, and endowment.

The question of the pope's position is somewhat complicated by the fact that he was probably the largest landowner in Italy. The "Patrimony of St. Peter," as it was called, comprised great estates in the Campagna, in Samnium, on the Adriatic coast, besides a considerable portion of Sicily. Any estimate of their extent and value can be only guess-work, but it is conjectured that in the time of Gregory the Great they would, if all massed together, have formed a district as large as Lancashire, and that the yearly revenue derived from them amounted to £420,000. It is to be observed that we are here dealing not with sovereignty but with ownership, and that the wide domains thus actually owned by the Bishop of Rome had probably been increased rather than diminished in the century and a half that had elapsed since the death of Gregory.

As to the purposes to which this vast wealth was applied, even a severe critic of the mediæval papacy must admit that they were, in the main, right and noble ones. We have no hint now of that nepotism which was the disgrace of the Roman see in much later ages. None of these early popes, as far as we know, ever "founded a family." The maintenance of the large and brilliant papal household was doubtless a first charge on the revenues of the see. The costly and somewhat ostentatious gifts of plate to St. Peter's Church, which are punctually recorded in the *Liber Pontificalis*, were perhaps a second charge upon them. But after all, a large proportion of these revenues must have gone towards the relief of poverty, sickness, and distress. The pope was now what the emperor had once been, the great relieving officer of Rome; not only in the Eternal City, but all over Italy, at any rate while such a pope as the first Gregory sat in St. Peter's chair, whenever a bishop brought a case of distress under his notice, there was a strong probability that he would receive a grant in aid from the papal revenues.

It is needless to point out what enormous power the ownership of such vast estates and the distribution of such princely revenues must have placed in the hands of the elderly ecclesiastic who was acclaimed as pope by the assembled multitude in the basilica of St. Peter. In the year 751 he was not yet a sovereign, but he was that kind of territorial magnate out of whom a sovereign might easily be made.

The curious and difficult relation which had subsisted

for so long between the three great powers in Italy was ended in 751, the year of Pippin's coronation, when Aistulf, King of the Lombards, captured the city of Ravenna and terminated the exarch's rule in Italy. Believing evidently that the time had come for the long postponed consolidation of Italy under the Lombard rule, he drew nigh to the city of Rome, and in some way or other threatened its independence. What he actually did it is difficult to discover from the verbose and passionate declamation of the papal biographer, but it seems clear that his soldiers committed some depredations on the "Patrimony of St. Peter," and it is probable that without laying formal siege to the city he threatened it with war unless the citizens would consent to pay him a poll-tax in acknowledgment of his sovereignty over them.

These depredations, or these schemes of conquest, were not needed to arouse the fierce and passionate hostility of the pope to the all-absorbing Lombard. So long as there had been three great powers in Italy there had been an equilibrium of a certain kind between them. In fact, the pope had more than once invoked the help of the Lombard, "unspeakable" as he called him, against his "most Christian" sovereign in Constantinople, when the latter pressed him too hard. But now the pope and the Lombard king stood face to face with no other rival to their greatness, and each of them probably felt, dimly but certainly, that it would be a duel to the death between them.

It was probably in the year 752, some months after the conquest of Ravenna, and when the hostile intentions of King Aistulf against Rome had been sufficiently

indicated, that Pope Stephen II. sent a secret message
by a pilgrim who had visited Rome, imploring the King
of the Franks to give him a formal invitation to his
court. In the spring of 753 the envoys of Pippin
brought the desired invitation, and a letter, in which
there was probably some promise of protection against
the Lombards. Just about the same time a messenger,
the *silentiarius* John, arrived from the Emperor Constantine V., desiring the pope to repair to the court of
Pavia and solicit King Aistulf to grant the restoration of
Ravenna to the empire. The pope had sent more than
one urgent message to the emperor imploring his protection, and this futile commission was the only reply.
The form of the despatch showed that the emperor still
regarded the pope as his subject, but its substance was
certainly some justification to Stephen for that transfer
of his allegiance from Constantine to Pippin, which had
now begun to present itself to his mind as a possible way
of escape from his difficulties. In itself the Imperial
Commission was not unwelcome, since it necessitated a
safe conduct from Aistulf for the journey to Pavia.

On the 13th of October, 753, Pope Stephen set forth
from Rome. Many of the Romans followed him out of
the gates, weeping and wailing, and striving in vain to
prevent him from undertaking the journey. But, though
weak in body, he had a stout heart, and was not to be
turned from his purpose. When he reached Pavia he
was met by the envoys of Aistulf, who brought him the
king's command not to mention the word restitution
in connection with Ravenna or the exarchate. He
answered boldly that no intimidation should procure
his silence on that subject. When admitted to the

royal presence he exhibited the gifts which he had
brought for the king, and, with many tears, implored
him to restore the captured cities to the empire. The
request was utterly vain; probably even the imperial
silentiarius, who was standing by, hardly expected that
it would be anything else. But then came another
request of much more serious import. Bishop Chrode-
gang and Duke Autchar, the high-born and powerful representatives of the King of the Franks, asked, in no obse-
quious tones, that the pope should be allowed to visit
their master. The pope was summoned to the royal
presence, and questioned as to his desire to cross the
Alps. Several of the officers of the court had been sent
to Stephen to warn him that he would incur the severe
displeasure of the king if he persisted in his project; but
when questioned by Aistulf himself, he boldly answered,
" If it be your will to relax my bonds, it is altogether
my will to undertake the journey." King Aistulf, we
are told, "gnashed his teeth like a lion." He knew too
well what danger this journey foreboded to himself and
the whole Lombard state, but the request, so made and
so supported, was one that he dared not refuse, and he
most reluctantly gave his consent. On the 15th of
November the pope started from Pavia, and travelled
rapidly lest Aistulf should after all seek to detain him.
When he reached Aosta he was already in Frankish
territory, though on the Italian side of the Alps. The
dangers which after that point terrified the pope and
his long train of trembling ecclesiastics were only the
dangers of nature's contriving, the steep cliffs and
impending avalanches of the Great St. Bernard; henceforth they were safe from the fear of man. Having

arrived at the great monastery of St. Maurice, in the valley of the Rhone, the pope and his followers rested there certain days. That had been the appointed place of meeting with the Frankish king, but apparently the impetuous old pope had reached it before he was expected.

"But the king," says the papal biographer, "hearing of the pope's arrival, went with great speed to meet him, together with his wife, his sons, and his chief nobles. For which purpose also he directed his son, named Carolus, to meet that quasi-angelic pope, together with some of his nobles. Then he himself, starting from his palace at Ponticum [Ponthieu], dismounted from his horse, and going three miles to meet him, with great humility prostrated himself before him on the ground, and so, together with his wife, sons, and nobles, received that most holy pope, to whom also he served the office of a groom, running for some distance by his stirrup. Then the aforesaid health-bringing man, with all his train, in a loud voice giving glory and ceaseless praises to Almighty God, marched to the palace, together with the king, with hymns and spiritual songs. This befell on the 6th day of January (754), on the most holy festival of the Epiphany."

This journey of the pope across the Alps is not only the first of a long and fateful series, but affords us our first glance at that young lad who was then only "the king's son Carolus," but who was one day to deal with popes on his own account, and was to be known, the world over, as *Carolus Magnus*. The date, as well as the place of his birth, is uncertain, but it is probable that he was born in 742, the year after his father's accession to the mayoralty, and was therefore under twelve years of age

when he was sent by his father to accompany Pope
Stephen II. on his journey of not less than 200 miles
from St. Maurice in Switzerland, to Ponthieu in
Champagne.

At the entry of the pope, the Frankish king had
humbled himself before him.   On the next day the
parts were reversed.   "The pope appeared, together
with his clerical companions, in the presence of Pippin.
Clothed in sackcloth, and with ashes on his head, he
cast himself on the ground, and besought the king, by
the mercies of Almighty God, and by the merits of the
blessed Apostles Peter and Paul, that he would free
himself and the Roman people from the hand of the
Lombards, and from slavery to the proud king Aistulf;
nor would he arise until King Pippin, together with his
sons and the nobles of the Franks, stretched forth their
hands and lifted him from the ground as a sign of their
future support and a pledge of his liberation."

There are some indications that the nobles and
warriors of the Frankish Court were averse to undertaking the risks and hardships of a Transalpine campaign, and it was probably for the sake of winning
their concurrence that this scene was enacted.   The
king, though not perhaps very eager in the cause, was
sufficiently bound to the pope by the memory of past
favours, and the hope of favours to come, in the shape
of papal blessings on his newly-assumed royalty.

The winter months of 754 were passed in embassies
between the two kings.   Pippin called upon Aistulf to
cease from his impious presumption, and to leave
unmolested the city of St. Peter and St. Paul.   His
ambassadors brought back naught but words of pride

and obstinacy from the Lombard. War was resolved on, but before it began, Pippin, mindful of the chances of war, and determined to secure the succession in his family, resolved to have another confirmation of his doubtful title from the hands of his venerable guest. Pope Stephen, who had passed the winter at the wealthy convent of St. Denis, "anointed the most pious Prince Pippin King of the Franks and Patrician of the Romans with the oil of holy anointing, according to the custom of the ancients, and at the same time crowned his two sons, who stood next him, in happy succession, namely, Charles and Carloman, with the same honour."

This passage is an important one, and we must pause upon it for a few minutes.

First, as to the rite of anointing. The writers who have most carefully enquired into the matter, are clear that this rite, though it had been practised upon the later Visigothic kings of Spain, and upon some of the British kings in Wales, was new to the Frankish monarchy, when performed first by Boniface and then by Stephen on the head of Pippin. It really rested upon Old Testament precedents, such as the anointings of Saul and of David: and it was possibly intended, as already hinted, to replace in some degree the religious sanction which in old heathen days royal families, such as the Merovingians, had possessed in their fabled descent from gods and demi-gods.

Secondly : as to the bestowal on Pippin of the title "Patrician of the Romans." Long ago, before the series of Western emperors came to an end, the word patrician had ceased to denote an aristocratic class, and had been used of a single powerful individual, otherwise called

"the Father of the Emperor," who in fact bore to the
sovereign a relation not unlike that which the Frankish
mayor of the palace bore to the Merovingian king.
Thus, in the fifth century, Aetius and Ricimer had
successively borne the dignity of patrician, and in the
sixth, the Ostrogothic king Theodoric, speaking by the
mouth of his minister Cassiodorus, had said, "The great
distinction of the patriciate is that it is a rank held for
life, like that of the priesthood from which it sprang.
The patrician takes precedence of all other dignities
save one, the consulship, and that is one which we ourselves sometimes assume. Since then, the imperial
lieutenant in Italy had apparently always assumed the
title of patrician at Rome, in addition to that of exarch
by which he was best known at Ravenna. Now that
the exarchs were gone, the sonorous and imposing title
might perhaps be said to be nobody's property. If any
one had a right to bestow it the emperor at Constantinople was the man : but he was far off and unpopular.
There was an obvious temptation to the Bishop of Rome
to pick the shining bauble out of the dust and present
it to his powerful friend on the other side of the Alps.
It is not likely that it included any definite functions of
government, but it probably carried with it, in a somewhat ill-defined and shadowy form, the right and the
duty of defending from external attacks the people and
city of Rome.

Thirdly : the pope included in his coronation-service
the two boyish sons of Pippin, Charles and Carloman,
and at the same time (if we may trust a curious memo-
randum, the *Clausula de Pippino*, which professes to have
been written in 767 and which is now generally con-

sidered authentic) the pope "blessed the Queen Bertrada
and the nobles of the Frankish nation, and while confirming them in the grace of the Holy Spirit, he bound
them under penalty of interdict and excommunication
never to presume to elect a king who should come forth
from the loins of any other than these persons whom
Divine Providence had raised to the throne, and who
through the intercession of the holy Apostles had been
consecrated and confirmed by the hands of their vicar,
the pope." Even so: that which had been done in the
case of the last Merovingian was never to be repeated
in the case of any Arnulfing however inefficient. The
ruler who four years ago was only king *de facto* must
now claim to the uttermost all the rights of a king *de jure*
descended from a long line of regal ancestors.

This solemn coronation of Pippin took place, we are
told, on the 28th of July 754. We naturally ask what
had so long delayed the intended expedition into Italy.
There had been a dangerous illness of the pope, the
result of the hardships of his journey and of the un-
accustomed rigours of a Gaulish winter. There had also
been more embassies: apparently Pippin would exhaust
all the resources of negotiation before he proceeded to
war. And lastly there had appeared at the royal villa
of Carisiacum an unexpected advocate to plead for the
Lombard king. This was none other than Pippin's
brother Carloman, lately ruler of Austrasia, and the
senior partner in the semi-royal firm, now a tonsured
monk, humbly though earnestly advocating the cause of
peace. The papal biographer sees in him only a dupe
tempted forth from his monastery by the "devilish persuasions of the unspeakable tyrant, Aistulf," and "striving

vehemently with all his might to subvert the cause of
God's Holy Church." Certainly this intervention of
the newly-made monk against the great Head and
Patron of all monks, is one of the strangest incidents in
his strange career : but it may be permitted us to conjecture that during his seven years' residence in Italy
he had acquired somewhat of an Italian heart and had
learnt to dread the ravages of

> "the arméd torrent poured
> Down the steep Alps."

Possibly too in the silence of his convent he had learned
to estimate at their true value the papal claims to
wealth and wide dominion, and with prophetic soul
foresaw that the armed interference of the Franks in
the quarrels of pope and Lombard king would in the
end bring good neither to the Church nor to his father's
house.

But whatever Carloman's motives might be, his inter-
position on behalf of Aistulf was firmly, perhaps un-
graciously, repelled. He was not allowed to return to
Italy, but was confined in a monastery in France, "where
after certain days," says the biographer, "at the call of
God he migrated from the light of day." He died on
the 17th of August 754. There is no suggestion of foul
play, and indeed Pippin's character, as far as we know
it, is too noble to warrant any such suggestion. It
seems probable that Carloman died broken-hearted at
the discovery that he had renounced the honest worldliness of the palace for the baser and more hypocritical
worldliness of the cloister and the cathedral.

After this episode of the intervention of Carloman,
his sons were shorn and sent to a convent. Grifo also,

as we have seen, perished a little before this time. There now remained only Pippin and his sons visibly before the world as representatives of the great Arnulfing House.

At last all negotiations were ended, and in the late summer Pippin with his whole army marched against Aistulf. He had reached S. Jean de Maurienne: the pass of Mont Cenis rose before him, by which he must make his way into Italy. He was still, however, on Frankish ground, for, as the result of the wars between Lombards and Franks two centuries previously, both Mont Cenis and (as has been already said) the Great St. Bernard with their adjacent towns of Susa and Aosta formed part of the Frankish kingdom. The Lombard king had come as far as Susa and had there accumulated great store of warlike machines, "for the nefarious defence of his kingdom against the republic and the Roman Apostolic see." He had, however, neglected the obvious precaution of sending soldiers forward to secure the heights and harass the Frankish army in their passage over the mountain. Thus it came to pass that a small but brave body of men, the advance-guard of Pippin's army, emerged unhindered into the valley of Susa. Thinking to win an easy victory Aistulf launched the Lombard host upon them. But the Franks, strong in their pious faith in God and St. Peter, and fighting also in a narrow valley, where the superior numbers of the enemy gave them no advantage, bravely repelled the Lombard onset. After Aistulf had seen many of his dukes and counts fall around him he turned to flee, and halted not till with few followers he had reached his capital of Pavia. Now was the path clear before the

Frankish king, who without difficulty crossed the
mountains, sacked the rich Lombard camp, laid waste
the valley of the Po with fire and sword, and appeared
with all his host under the walls of Pavia. After some
days Aistulf sounded the trumpet for parley, and sought
terms of peace. This was granted to him on condition
of his paying 30,000 solidi (£18,000) to Pippin and
promising to restore to the papacy all the estates which
he had torn from the papal patrimony and to live
henceforth at peace with the successor of St. Peter, who
had by this time returned to Rome. Possibly there was
also included in the terms of this peace the far more
important condition that he should surrender to the pope
the Pentapolis and the cities of Ceccano and Narni in
the neighbourhood of Rome, as well as pay a yearly
tribute of 5000 solidi (£3000) to the Frankish king.

Though hostages had been given and solemn oaths
sworn for the performance of these conditions, the
Lombard king did not keep, perhaps had never intended
to keep them. Narni indeed was handed over to the
pope, but apparently none of the other cities or lands
which Aistulf had promised to restore; and on New
Year's day 756 he appeared with a large army before
the gates of Rome. The men of Tuscany blockaded
the gate of St. Peter's; the Beneventans, the gates of St.
Paul and St. John Lateran; while Aistulf himself, like
another Alaric, appeared before the Salarian gate and
called upon the citizens as they valued their lives, to
open the gate and hand over the pontiff to his tender
mercies. For nearly two months had the siege lasted
when Stephen II. contrived, through the agency of the
abbot Warnehar, to make audible to Pippin his piteous

cries for help.   In the last and most urgent of these
letters the pope associates St. Peter with himself, repre-
sents the Apostle as praying Pippin to hasten his aid,
"lest you should allow this city of Rome to perish,
in which the Lord has appointed that my body should
rest, and which He has commended to my protection
and made the foundation of the faith."   This letter
is certainly a very daring rhetorical artifice, but it is
probable that it was understood to be that and nothing
more, both by the sender and the receiver.

This time the Frankish king required but little per-
suasion. The flagrant breach of the treaty made with himself, as well as with the pope, was an insult which called
for vengeance.   In the spring of 756 he put his army in
motion, and after a rapid march by way of Chalons and
Geneva he was once more under the snows of Mont
Cenis. The Lombard soldiers again failed to prevent
his passage over the crest of the pass, and when he had
descended into the higher valleys where they were
stationed, the Franks, who had evidently among them
many trained mountaineers (no doubt from the regions
now known as Dauphiné, Savoy, and Switzerland) turned
the position of the Lombards by mountain tracks which
they had left unguarded, and descending upon them
with that *furia Francese* of which in a later day
Italy was to have so many and such fatal examples,
slew a multitude of the enemy and put the rest to flight.
Again was all the upper valley of the Po devastated by
the Frankish troops, and again did Pippin pitch his
tents on either side of the Ticino under the walls of
Pavia.   At the sight thereof, Aistulf, abandoning all
hope of successful resistance, obtained the mediation of

the nobles and bishops in the invading army, and, imploring pardon for his broken promises, submitted to the conditions, hard as they were, imposed by the conqueror. These were, the surrender to Pippin of one third of the royal hoard stored up through many generations at Pavia, the bestowal of large presents on the nobles of the Frankish court, the payment of long arrears of tribute, and, now at length in very deed, the cession of the cities of the exarchate and the Pentapolis.

But to whom were these cities, wrested as they had been by the Lombards from the representative of the Eastern Emperor, to be ceded? That was a question which, though it had probably been discussed and decided by the Pope and the King of the Franks, had not received a definite answer in the face of Europe till this summer of 756. It happened that at the very time when Pippin was opening his campaign, there arrived in Rome, George and John, Chief Secretary and Captain of the Guard, from the Emperor Constantine V. on a mission to the Frankish king. Journeying by sea to Marseilles, and then crossing the Alps, the Secretary found Pippin under the walls of Pavia, and entreated him with much earnestness and with the promise of many gifts from the emperor, to hand over the city of Ravenna and the other cities of the exarchate to the imperial rule. "But not thus," says the papal biographer, "did he avail to bend the strong will of that most Christian and most benign man, so loyal to God and such a lover of St. Peter, King Pippin, to hand over those cities to the imperial dominion; for that devout and most mild-mannered king declared that never should those cities be alienated from the power of St. Peter, and the rights of the Roman Church and the pontiff of the Apostolic see : affirming with an oath that not to win the favour of any mortal man had he twice addressed himself to the fight, but solely for love of St. Peter and for the pardon of his sins : and vowing too that no amount of money should induce him to take away what he had once given to St. Peter. With this answer he gave the imperial messenger leave to return to his country by another way, and he having failed in his commission returned to Rome."

This is apparently the critical point from which we must date the pope's independence of the Eastern, or as we ought still to call him, the Roman Emperor. Up to this time, whatever divergencies there may have been in doctrine or in policy, the Bishop of Rome has always been in theory the subject of the Emperor of Rome. Now he distinctly asserts, by the mouth of his powerful friend from over the Alps, that certain broad domains which have been conquered from the empire, shall be handed over not to the emperor but to himself. He shakes himself loose from his old subjection and becomes by the same act a sovereign prince, not only—and this is an important point—in the newly-acquired territory of the exarchate, but also in his old home of the *Ducatus Romae.*

The cities now handed over to the see of Rome were twenty-two in number, and stretched along the Adriatic coast from the mouths of the Po to within a few miles of Ancona and inland as far as the Apennines. The plenipotentiary of the Frankish king, Fulrad, Abbot of St. Denis, travelled through the Pentapolis, and the exarchate, together with Aistulf's commissioner, entered each city, received its keys and was introduced to the chief magistrates, who journeyed onward in his train. All these arrived at Rome. The local magistrates were doubtless presented to their new sovereign. The keys of Ravenna and all the other cities were laid on St. Peter's tomb along with the donation by which King Pippin granted them for ever to St. Peter and the pope. This done Abbot Fulrad returned to Paris having accomplished his world-historical mission. Stephen II., 94th Bishop of Rome, was now in fact not only pope but king, and a beginning was made of those "States of the Church" which with one brief interval have down to our own day intersected the map of Italy.

I have dwelt at considerable length on Pippin's relations with the papacy, because they are inseparably connected with the most important event in the history of his son. His other achievements, though remarkable, and though they were evidently much nearer to his heart (for his intervention in Italian affairs was done grudgingly and almost against his will), must be dismissed in a few words.

In the first place, in the year 759 a Frankish army besieged Narbonne. A solemn oath was sworn to the Goths, that if they would surrender the city to Pippin they should be allowed to keep their own separate laws, and on this the Goths rose, slew the Saracens who held the city for the Caliph of Cordova, and handed it over to the Frankish generals. With this capture ended the Moslem domination in Southern Gaul, though it was not the last time that the turbans of the Moors were to be seen north of the Pyrenees.

The conditions upon which the Christian inhabitants

of Narbonne consented to help the Frankish host against the Saracens, show how strong was still the spirit of separate Gothic nationality in that part of Gaul. Something of the same spirit, blended with other elements, tended to make all that great region south and west of the Loire, which went by the name of Aquitaine, seek for independence from the Franks whom she still looked upon as strangers and foreigners. We have seen how this spirit of independence was working when Eudo was Duke of Aquitaine and Charles Martel *major domus* of Francia, and how it was only the pressure of a terrible danger which caused Eudo to seek the help of Charles before the battle of Poitiers. Eudo was succeeded (735) by his son Hunold, who seven years after, on the death of Charles Martel, strove to throw off the Frankish yoke, but soon found that what the father had won his two sons were well able to maintain. In 744 Hunold, by false oaths, enticed into his power his brother Hatto, who apparently aspired to share his dominion, put out his eyes and thrust him into prison. Then, apparently in penitence for this crime, he, like Carloman, retired into a monastery and was succeeded in his duchy by his son Waifar.

This Waifar, Duke of Aquitaine, is a man of whom we would gladly know more, but of whose deeds no song or saga has preserved the memory. Only a few dry sentences in chronicles, written by the flatterers of his foe, tell us that for nine years (760-768) King Pippin carried on with him a war which, beginning with complaints about the withholding of the revenues of some Frankish churches, was more and more embittered as time went on, and in the end became nothing less than a struggle for the absolute subjugation of Aquitaine and the destruction of the dynasty of Eudo. In 768 the Frankish king took the mother, sister, and nieces of Waifar prisoners in the town of Saintes. Still the chief fugitive escaped him. In the forests of Perigord, among the mountain-caves of the Dordogne where, ages before, neolithic man had graven the likeness of the reindeer and the bear, the grandson of Eudo made his ever-changing hiding-places. At length the warriors of Pippin dividing themselves into four bands ran him to earth somewhere in Saintonge. He was at once put to death, and the dream of an independent Aquitaine vanished.

While Pippin was labouring over the work, so necessary from his point of view, of the subjugation of Aquitaine, Bavaria, which held a somewhat similar position of semi-independence on the south-east of the kingdom, was escaping from his grasp. The work of the reconquest of this great duchy had to be left to his sons, and I must postpone to a future chapter the story of the changing fortunes of Tassilo, Duke of Bavaria.

It was while tarrying at Saintes and celebrating his triumph over Waifar that Pippin was attacked by his last and fatal sickness. In vain did he visit the shrines of St. Martin at Tours and St. Denis at Paris. The hand of death was upon him, and having convoked all the nobles, dukes, and counts of the Franks, and all the bishops and chief ecclesiastics of the kingdom to an assembly at Paris, he there solemnly, " with the consent of his chiefs," divided his dominions between his two sons, Charles and Carloman. He then after a few days died (24th September 768) and was buried at St. Denis

with great pomp. He had governed the people of the
Franks either as *major domus* or as king for twenty-six
years, and he had probably reached about the 54th year
of his age. The princes of the Arnulfing line, though
not like the debauched and short-lived Merovings,
seldom saw the end of their sixth decade of life.

What Pippin did for the foundation of the monarchy
which was to be the basis of the new settlement of
Europe, was in its way quite as important and even more
enduring than that which was done by his more
illustrious son, upon whose reign we now enter.

CHAPTER V

THE situation of affairs after the death of Pippin seems at first sight almost the exact counterpart of that which existed at the death of Charles Martel. We have again two brothers ruling, one of them a Carloman, and the Frankish dominions are divided between them. There are however some important differences. In the first place the two young princes are now not mere *majores domus* but acknowledged kings. Moreover, the division of the Frankish territories between the brothers proceeds on a different principle from that adopted in 741. The dividing line then ran north and south: now it is more nearly east and west. Thus Charles, the elder son, again has Austrasia and the North German lands dependent upon it, but probably also the larger part of Neustria; while Burgundy, Provence, and Alamannia (Swabia) fall to the lot of Carloman. Aquitaine, which Pippin looked upon as his own conquest, was probably included in Charles's portion. But the general tendency of this division, even more perhaps than of the division of 741, must have been to give the lands where the memories of Roman civilisation were strong and where the Latin tongue was used, to the younger brother, and all the specially Teutonic, Frankish lands, the cradle of the Arnulfing race, to the elder.

Another, and what might have been a more important difference between the two partitions lay in the relation between the brothers. So long as the partnership lasted between the elder Carloman and Pippin they appear to have lived in mutual loyalty and love : but the relation between Charles and the younger Carloman was one of scarcely veiled enmity. Their mother, the good and clever queen Bertrada did her best to keep the peace between them, but some of Carloman's friends fanned the flame of discord. Dislike might have broken out into actual civil war but for the opportune death of Carloman, which occurred on the 4th of December 771, after a little more than three years of joint sovereignty. This Carloman is a much less strongly marked figure than his uncle and namesake, and in fact, the quarrel with his far more famous brother, and his marriage to a noble Frankish maiden named Gerberga, are almost the only events in his life that history records.

On hearing the tidings of his brother's death, Charles at once proceeded to the villa of Corbonacus near Soissons which had probably been Carloman's chief residence, and there, with the consent of Archbishop Wiltchar, of Fulrad, Abbot of St. Denis and royal chaplain, and of some of the nobles of Carloman's court, he was solemnly proclaimed King of all the Franks. The claims of the two infant sons of Carloman were thus set aside, it would seem, rather by the influence of the great ecclesiastics of the realm than with the hearty consent of the nobles, some of whom shared the exile of the widowed

Gerberga, who with her children crossed the Alps and sought shelter at the Court of the King of the Lombards. We may probably discern in this action of Wiltchar and Fulrad somewhat of the same statesman-like spirit which caused the great Anglo-Saxon churchmen to work for the consolidation of the Heptarchy into one kingdom. None knew better than they the evils which a long minority and protracted dissensions between north and south would bring upon the kingdom, and for the safety of the state they were perhaps justified in encouraging Charles to seize the auspicious moment for reuniting the divided realm.

When Charles thus became sole ruler of the Frankish state he was probably a little under thirty years of age. He was a man of commanding presence, more than six feet high, with large and lustrous eyes, a rather long nose, a bright and cheerful countenance and a fine head of hair, which we may suppose to have been now yellow like that of his Teutonic forefathers, though when his biographer Einhard knew him best it had the beautiful whiteness of age.

Already in the three years of the joint kingship he had had some experience of war. Though his father seemed to have thoroughly subdued Aquitaine, the embers of disaffection were still smouldering there, and on the appearance of a certain Hunold, probably of the family of the well-remembered Eudo, they broke out into a flame (769). Charles, having vainly called on his brother Carloman for aid, marched to Angoulême, where he concentrated his forces. On his appearance the insurrection collapsed and Hunold had a narrow escape of capture. By his superior knowledge of the country he succeeded in baffling his pursuers and made his way into Gascony. Lupus, duke of that region, was minded to give him shelter, but on receiving a message from Charles that if the fugitive were not surrendered he would march his army into Gascony and not depart thence till he had thoroughly subdued it to his obedience, the Gascon duke lost heart and surrendered Hunold and his wife to their conqueror. We hear nothing more of their fate. Gascony, unlike Aquitaine, kept its duke, and though it must have vaguely recognised the over-lordship of Charles, it was probably the least thoroughly subdued and assimilated of all the regions of that which we now call France.

But meanwhile the whole current of events— marriages, deaths, worldly ambition and ghostly counsel —was sweeping Charles onward to the great exploit of his reign, the conquest of Italy. When we last glanced at Italian affairs we saw Abbot Fulrad, together with the commissioner of the Lombard king Aistulf, gathering up the keys of the cities of the exarchate and bringing them to lay at the feet of Pope Stephen II. That important event, the beginning of the temporal dominion of the pope, occurred in 756, twelve years before the accession of Charles. In the interval many changes had occurred, and several new actors had appeared upon the scene.

In the first place, only a month or two after he had performed the long-delayed surrender of the exarchate, Aistulf died. His death was due to an accident in the hunting-field, but as he had been so often at war with the Church, of course the papal biographer sees in it "a blow from the Divine hand." Desiderius, Duke of

Tuscany, now aimed at the Lombard crown: but
Ratchis, the long since dethroned king, emerged from
his convent and succeeded in reigning once more for
three months as King of the Lombards. Desiderius,
however, sought the intervention of the pope—probably
the return of the monk Ratchis to secular life was dis-
approved of on religious grounds—and by the promise
of adding yet more cities to the new papal dominions
succeeded in procuring his powerful interference on his
behalf. Abbot Fulrad, too, that able *chargé d'affaires* of
the Frankish king, exerted himself on the same side,
probably threatening his master's intervention. The
result of the negotiations was that the matter was settled,
apparently without bloodshed. Ratchis stepped back
into his convent, Desiderius surrendered the cities for
which the pope had bargained, and became King—as it
proved the last native king—of the Lombards (March
757). In the following month Pope Stephen II. died,
and was succeeded by his brother Paul I. The ten
years of this prelate's pontificate seem to have been a
time of comparative peace between pope and Lombard
king. Then came a stormy interregnum, the invasion
of the papal see by an intrusive Tuscan nobleman, his
expulsion after thirteen months, and the elevation to
the papal chair of the Sicilian, Stephen III. We need
not here enter into the history of these obscure revolutions in which two parties, a Lombard and a Frankish,
are dimly seen struggling for the mastery. We note
only that Stephen III.'s elevation (7th August 768)
happened but a few months before the death of Pippin.
About two years after, we find him addressing an extraordinary letter full of passionate animosity against the

Lombards, to the two young Frankish kings. He has heard that Desiderius King of the Lombards is seeking to persuade one or other of the royal brothers to dismiss his lawfully wedded wife and marry a Lombard princess, his daughter. Perish the thought! To say nothing of the impiety of putting away a wedded wife to marry another woman, what folly, what madness it would be in the kings of so noble and illustrious a nation as the Franks to pollute themselves by marrying a woman of the stinking Lombard race, which is not counted in the number of the nations, and from which it is certain that the brood of lepers has sprung! "Remember and consider that ye have been anointed with holy oil with celestial benediction by the hands of the vicar of St. Peter, and take care that you do not become entangled in such crimes. Remember, too, that you have promised the blessed Peter, his vicar [Pope Stephen II.] and his successors that you would be friends to his friends and enemies to his enemies, as we have promised to you the like and do firmly continue therein. How, then, can you escape the guilt of perjury if you ally yourselves with that perjured nation of the Lombards, who, for ever attacking the Church of God and invading this our province of the Romans, are proved to be our deadliest foes?"

This passionate, almost insolent letter of dissuasion was of no avail. Carloman indeed kept his wedded wife Gerberga, but Charles, some time in the year 770, put away his wife, a noble Frankish lady, named Himiltruda, and married the daughter of Desiderius, whom his mother Bertrada, a friend of the Lombard alliance, had brought back with her from Italy after a pilgrimage to the tombs of the Apostles.

The tie of kinship between Frank and Lombard, thus formed, was soon and rudely broken. After a year of wedlock the daughter of Desiderius was back again in her father's court a divorced and rejected wife (771). What were the motives of her husband for such insulting treatment of his young queen none of his contemporaries have told us. The monk of St. Gall, writing a century after the event, tells us that the lady was a delicate invalid, unlikely ever to become a mother, and that for this reason Charles, acting by the advice of his most saintly bishops, put her away as if she were dead. It is a plausible conjecture that the king, remembering the passionate endeavour of the pope to dissuade him from this marriage, may have recognised a Divine judgment in its threatened sterility, and may for that reason have decided on ending it.

This harsh termination of an alliance on which Queen Bertrada had set her heart, and which she had been the chief agent in bringing to pass, caused, for the time, an estrangement between mother and son, the only one, we are told, that ever took place between them.

The repudiation of the Lombard princess of course did not improve the relations between Desiderius and Charles. Still more strained did those relations become when, on the death of Carloman, a few months later, his widow, with her infant children and some trusty adherents crossed the Alps and placed herself under the protection of the Lombard king. Charles, we are told, considered this proceeding on the part of his sister-in-law to be "superfluous," but nevertheless bore it patiently. The year 772 was fully occupied with the first of those great campaigns against the Saxons which will form the subject of a later chapter; and Charles had no time or energy to spare for the complicated affairs of Italy.

But during that year (772) these Italian complications were rapidly increasing. At the end of January came the death of Pope Stephen III., the Sicilian, a weak and ineffectual man, who during all his short pontificate had been pulled this way and that by the two factions, the Lombard and the Frankish, which divided the nobility of Rome. When his insolent letter to Charles failed to divert him from the Lombard alliance, he had thrown himself into the arms of Desiderius, and allowed the Lombard faction, headed by a certain Paulus Afiarta, to work their lawless will in Rome, banishing, blinding, imprisoning, putting to death the chiefs of the opposite party.

Now, however, on the death of the Sicilian, a very different man was raised to the vacant papal chair. This was Hadrian I., a man of Roman birth, of spotless if somewhat ambitious character, capable of forming and executing large and statesmanlike plans, a man not altogether unworthy in point of intellect to be compared to the great Emperor whose name he bore. His pontificate, one of the longest in the papal annals, lasted very nearly twenty-four years (772-795), so that he narrowly missed "seeing the years of St. Peter," and during this long space of time, common hopes, common dangers, common enterprises drew him and Charles sometimes very close together, and though there were also some sharp disputes between them, the king, we are told, "regarded the pope as his chief friend, and when he received the tidings of his death wept for him as for a much loved son or brother."

As soon as Hadrian assumed the pontifical robe it was manifest to all men that the unnatural friendship between pope and Lombard king had come to an end. The prison doors were opened for the anti-Lombard partisans, the civil and military officers who had been driven into exile were recalled. Paulus Afiarta himself was tried and put to death by the Archbishop of Ravenna. Hadrian indeed seems to have exerted himself that the sentence might be commuted to banishment, but there is no doubt that he thoroughly approved of criminal proceedings of some kind being taken against the great unscrupulous Lombard partizan.

The action of Desiderius at this eventful crisis of his nation's history is not easy to understand : it is only possible here to describe its general course without entering into details. He seems to have recognised that he had an enemy in the new pope and one of a more determined kind than either Paul I. or Stephen III., whose demands for a further cession of territory he had been for the last fifteen years successfully evading. Apparently, however, he cherished the hope that by a judicious mixture of threats and entreaties he might draw the pope over to his side and induce him to anoint the infant sons of Carloman as Kings of the Franks. For to this desperate act of defiance to Charles was he now impelled both by the memory of his daughter's wrongs and by the conviction that, sooner or later, war must again break out between the Frank and the Lombard. In this frame of mind he despatched alternately embassies to sue for the pope's friendship and armies to invade his territory. The rapid changes of his attitude probably irritated the pontiff then as much as they perplex

the historian to-day. First Faenza, Ferrara, and Com-
acchio, the latest acquisitions of the papacy, were
occupied; then Ravenna was closely pressed; Urbino
and the greater part of the Pentapolis were invaded;
Blera and Otriculum, not a day's journey from Rome,
were entered by the Lombard troops, who in the former
city are said to have perpetrated a cruel massacre of
the unresisting inhabitants. But all these violent
measures failed to shake the resolution of Hadrian or
induce him to consent to an interview with Desiderius.
His uniform answer to the Lombard ambassadors was,
"First let your master restore the possessions of which
he has unjustly despoiled St. Peter; and then, but not
till then, will I grant him an interview."

At last, when the Lombard king was evidently preparing to tighten his grip on Rome itself, Pope Hadrian
sent a messenger named Peter to beg for the help of the
great King of the Franks. At the same time he did
what he could to put the city in a state of defence,
gathering in soldiers from Tuscany, Campania, and the
Pentapolis, removing the most precious adornments of
the churches of St. Peter and St. Paul to safer custody
within the walls of the city, and barring up all the doors
of St. Peter's so that the Lombard king, without some
violent act of sacrilege, should not be able to enter.

At last, in February or March 773, Peter the papal
messenger (having travelled by sea to Marseilles, as all
the land routes were beset by Lombard soldiers) arrived
at Theodo's villa where Charles was holding his court.
This is the place which the Neustrian citizens of the
French Republic still call Thionville, while the Austrasian
subjects of Kaiser Wilhelm, who have wrested it from

the Neustrians, speak of it as Diedenhofen. It is now a strong border fortress on the Moselle, sixteen miles north of Metz. Hither, then, came the papal messenger to utter his master's piteous cry for help. Probably the ambassadors of Desiderius appeared there also to deny the charges brought against him, or to declare that whatever he had forcibly taken from the papal see he had already surrendered. Charles resolved on war if war was needful, but, even as his father Pippin had done, he tried diplomacy first. Three messengers, a bishop, an abbot, and a courtier, were sent to Italy to enquire into the rights of the quarrel, and on their return and report that the cities violently taken from St. Peter were not restored, Charles, still treading in his father's footsteps, sent one more embassy to Desiderius, offering the Lombard 14,000 golden solidi (£8000) if he would restore the conquered cities, and fully satisfy all the Papal demands. The offer was refused, and Charles having summoned the Frankish host to his standard, set forward for Italy.

According to a plan which he frequently adopted, and one reason for which was probably the desire to lessen the difficulties of commissariat, Charles, after mustering his troops at Geneva, divided his host into two parts—one of which under his uncle Bernard was to cross by the Great St. Bernard and to descend upon Aosta, while the other which he himself commanded, crossing the Mont Cenis, was to take the road to Susa. Both divisions, as in his father's time, traversed the highest points of their respective passes without hindrance, but when Charles descended into the long and narrow valley of the Dora Susa, he found his further progress barred by the fortifications and the army of Desiderius. He renewed his offers of a money payment in return for the papal cities, he even expressed his willingness to be satisfied with a mere promise to surrender those cities, if three Lombard nobles were handed over to him as hostages; but all was in vain. Strong in the impregnability of his fortifications Desiderius refused every offer of accommodation, until a sudden panic seized his host, the fortresses were abandoned, and again, as in Pippin's time, all the Lombard army retreated down the valley and shut itself up behind the walls of Pavia.

So sudden and scarce hoped for a termination to what looked like an evenly balanced game was naturally attributed by the papal biographer to a divinely inspired terror; but a Frankish chronicler tells us of a picked squadron of troops which Charles had sent over an unguarded pass, and later local tradition spoke of a certain Lombard minstrel who for a brilliant reward guided the Frankish troops by untrodden ways to the rear of his countrymen's position. We know from other evidence that there were Lombards who were disaffected to Desiderius, and had opened negotiations with the Frankish king; but the story of treachery in this case is not well vouched for. It is possible that Bernard's successful transit over the pass which preserves the memory of his namesake saint, may have turned the rear of the Lombard position, and compelled Desiderius to seek safety in flight.

The siege of Pavia, which was now formed by Charles, began probably about the end of September 773, and lasted for ten months. The other great focus of

Lombard resistance was the city of Verona, where
Adelchis, son of Desiderius, commanded the garrison,
and where those important guests Gerberga, widow of
Carloman, her children and her trusty counsellor Autchar
had taken refuge. Thither, Charles proceeded at an
early period of the siege of Pavia. The resistance seems
to have been slight, perhaps the garrison half-hearted.
Very soon after Charles's arrival, Gerberga and her
train came forth from the city and surrendered themselves
to his will. The city itself was probably surrendered at
the same time; and the young prince Adelchis made
his escape to Constantinople. After this point the
widow and children of Carloman vanish from the scene.
We should certainly have been informed if any of them
had been put to death, and we may therefore safely
assume that Charles was merciful. There are faint and
doubtful traces of one of the sons as holding the bishopric
of Nice.

Charles appears to have spent his Christmas under
canvas before the walls of Pavia, or else in one of the
numerous expeditions by which he brought the cities on
the left bank of the Po into his obedience. But as the
siege still dragged on, though there could be little doubt
of its final event, when Easter approached, Charles, with
a brilliant train of dukes and counts, of bishops and
abbots, journeyed through Tuscany to Rome. Never
had his father, King Pippin, though he had twice crossed
the Alps, visited the Eternal City, and this was Charles's
first visit to that Rome with which his name was to be
inseparably linked in after ages. He went by forced
marches, hastening to be in Rome on the eve of Easter
Sunday. At thirty miles from the city, Pope Hadrian

ordered that he should be met by the nobles of the
Ducatus Romae, displaying the banner of St. Peter. At
one mile from the city the various squadrons of the
Roman militia with their officers and the boys out of
the schools met him, all bearing palm-branches and
olive-branches and crosses, and singing loud his praises,
for Hadrian had ordered that in all things the reception
of the King of the Franks should do him as great honour
as ever had been done of old to the patrician and
exarch arriving from Ravenna. When Charles saw the
crosses and the banners he dismounted from his horse,
and went on foot with all his nobles to the church
of St. Peter. There on the top of the steps stood Pope
Hadrian, with all the clergy and people of Rome who
had risen at dawn to be ready to welcome the victorious
king. As he ascended each step, Charles knelt down
and kissed the venerable stones; and so he reached the
summit where, in the long *atrium* outside the doors of
the church the pope stood waiting to receive him.
King and pontiff were clasped in mutual embrace (we
hear nothing of the abject prostrations performed by
later emperors before later popes), and then holding
Hadrian's right hand Charles entered the great basilica,
while all the clergy and all the monks shouted with
loud voices, "Blessed is he that cometh in the name of
the Lord." Then the king and all the Frankish nobles
and churchmen in his train knelt at the tomb of St.
Peter, thanking God for the great victories already
wrought through the intervention of the Prince of the
Apostles. On the three following days, at Sta. Maria
Maggiore, at St. Peter's and St. Paul's, the king, after
humbly imploring the papal permission, offered up his

prayers to God, and on Easter Sunday there was a
great banquet at the Lateran. Thus we come to the
Wednesday on which an important piece of business
was transacted between the two potentates. So much
here turns on a few words that it will be well to give
a literal translation of the passage in the *Liber Pontificalis* (our only authority), which describes this memorable interview.

" On the fourth day of the week, the pope, with his
staff of officers, both civil and ecclesiastical, went forth to
the church of St. Peter, and there meeting the king in
conference, earnestly prayed him, and with paternal
affection exhorted him, to fulfil in its entirety that promise which his father, the late King Pippin of blessed
memory, had made, and which he himself with his
brother Carloman and all the nobles of France had confirmed to St. Peter and his vicar Pope Stephen II.,
when he visited Frankland, that they would grant
divers cities and territories in that province of Italy
to St. Peter and his vicars for a perpetual possession.
And when he (Charles) had caused that promise which
was made in Frankland in a place called Carisiacum to
be read over to him, all its contents were approved by
himself and his nobles. And of his own accord, with
good and willing mind, that most excellent and most
Christian king Charles caused another promise of gift like
the first to be drawn up by Etherius his chaplain and
notary, and in this he granted the same cities and territories to St. Peter and promised that they should be
conveyed to the pope with their boundaries set forth as is
contained in the aforesaid donation, to wit : From Luna
with the island of Corsica, thence to Surianum, thence

to Mons Bardonis (that is Vercetum), thence to Parma,
thence to Rhegium, and from thence to Mantua and
Mons Silicis, and moreover the whole exarchate of
Ravenna such as it was of old time, and the provinces of
Venetia and Istria: moreover the whole duchies of
Spoletium and Beneventum."

The papal biographer then goes on to describe the
signing of this donation by Charles himself with all his
bishops, abbots, dukes, and counts, its being laid upon
the altar of St. Peter, and afterwards placed within his
tomb, and the "terrible oath" which was sworn by all
the signers, promising to St. Peter and Pope Hadrian that
they would keep all the promises contained in the
document.

Let us look at the extent of the territories which
according to the papal biographer were thus conveyed
to the Roman pontiff. The island of Corsica: that is
clear, though introduced in a curious connection. Then
the line starts from the coast of Italy, just at the point
where the Genoese and Tuscan territory join: it crosses
the Apennines and strikes the Po a little north of
Parma. From Mantua it works round to the head of
the Adriatic and includes the peninsula of Istria. The
exarchate of Ravenna, "as it was of old time," reached
inland to the Apennines and probably is here to be
taken as including the Pentapolis. The extent of the
two great Lombard duchies of Spoleto and Benevento is
perfectly well known; they included the whole of Italy
south of Ancona except the duchy of Rome, a little
territory round Naples and the district which is now
called Calabria in the extreme south, the toe of Italy.

Instead, therefore, of asking what this donation included, it is more to the purpose to enquire what it excluded. As the duchy of Rome is apparently treated as already an undoubted part of the papal dominions, we may say, using modern geographical terms, that if this donation had ever been carried into effect the popes would have become sovereigns of the whole of Italy except the Riviera, Piedmont, part of Lombardy north of the Po, the city of Naples, and Calabria.

It is almost impossible to believe that Charles, even in the fervour caused by his first visit to Rome, his meeting with St. Peter's vicar, and his prayers in the great Roman basilicas, can have meant to convey such vast territories as these to an ecclesiastic, however eminent, whose pretensions to rank as a civil ruler of any territory, however small, were only twenty years old. It is absolutely impossible to believe that his father can (as is here implied) have promised to endow the pope with territories such as those of Venetia and Istria, which were in no sense Lombard, and were still in close connection with the Eastern Empire. The whole subsequent course of history shows that Charles, with all his lavish generosity to the Holy See, never seriously contemplated making its occupant the virtual lord of Italy.

What solution of the enigma is possible ? The idea of an absolute fabrication of the document naturally occurs to the mind, especially to the mind of a student who is constantly confronted with charters forged in the interests of some church or monastery. This is the view taken by many modern enquirers, amongst others by Malfatti (the careful author of "Imperatori e Papi"), who inclines to assign the fabrication of the document to the ninth century, "famous for so many other fictions of that kind."

On the other hand, Abbé Duchesne, the learned and impartial editor of the *Liber Pontificalis*, declares that he looks upon this passage as the work of an absolutely contemporary author, and that he cannot accept the theory of a later fabrication. At the same time he fully admits that this vast cession of territory to the pope never took practical effect, and he suggests that somewhere about 781 the pope, finding that there was no chance of realising the splendid dream of sovereignty over the whole of Italy in which he had indulged at the interview of 774, liberated Charles from the promises then made, in consideration of some important addition to the duchy of Rome over which his rule was undisputed. In point of fact we find at that time the pope unable to maintain himself even in the territory of the exarchate, which was wrested from him by the ambitious Archbishop of Ravenna. Prudence may therefore have suggested to him the expediency of concentrating his attention on the duchy of Rome, and at least strengthening the frontiers of that possession.

Another theory for which some good arguments may be adduced, is that in this promised gift we are still dealing not with a grant of sovereignty but with a restitution of property ; that for instance when Spoleto and Benevento are mentioned, all that Charles undertook, or at least meant to undertake, was that any "patrimonies" in either of those duchies of which the see of St. Peter had been unjustly despoiled by the Lombards should be restored to it.

It is not for the present author to pretend to decide

a question on which so many able scholars are at issue,
and to which so many special treatises have been
devoted ; but the impression produced on his mind is
that at least the hand of the interpolator, if not that
of the wholesale fabricator, must have been at work in
the passage which he has quoted from the *Liber Pontificalis*.

Having finished his conferences with the Pope, in
which he discussed with him many matters ecclesiastical
as well as civil, Charles returned to his camp under the
walls of Pavia. It was now the tenth month of the
siege : disease and probably famine were pressing the
defenders hard : and Desiderius, who had never been a
popular sovereign, heard on every side of the defection
of his countrymen. At length on a certain Tuesday in
June (774) the city opened her gates to her conqueror.
The great hoard was handed over, the nobles and chief
men from all the cities of northern Italy came to
Charles seated in the royal palace of Pavia, and acknowledged him as their lord : the dominion of the
Lombards in Italy was at an end.

To Desiderius and his family Charles showed himself
merciful in his triumph. The fallen king was carried
across the Alps, accompanied by his wife and one daughter
(whether this was the divorced wife of Charles we know
not), and was invited to enter the seclusion of a monastery, in Austrasia, where, if any faith is to be placed in
the stories that were current a century or two after his
death, he devoted himself with assiduity to the duties
of the cloister, and even declared that he would not
desire to resume his crown, having entered the service
of the King of Kings.

Very soon after the capture of Pavia, Charles was

back again on the Rhine, as the affairs of North
Germany required his immediate attention. It was
perhaps in part from the scantiness of his leisure,
but it was surely in part also from his statesmanlike
insight into the conditions of the problem before him,
that he made so little change in the internal constitution of his new kingdom. There was no attempt to
amalgamate the regions north and south of the Alps:
Italy did not become a part of "Francia," but Charles
took his place as successor of the long line of kings
from Alboin to Desiderius who had reigned over
Lombard Italy. "Rex Francorum et Langobardorum
atque Patricius Romanorum" : that was now his full title.
As King of the Franks he ruled the wide regions north
of the Alps: as King of the Lombards he ruled all of
Italy that the Lombards had once held: as Patrician of
the Romans he seems to have been recognised as supreme
ruler of all the rest of Italy except the little fragments
on the coast which still held by their allegiance to the
eastern emperor.

What, then, during the years of transition between
774 and 800, were his relations to that eastern emperor?
Some answer to this question will be given in a subsequent chapter. And what were his relations to the
pope, in those territories in which his or his father's
donation had taken effect? A question almost impossible to answer. Never was there a more striking
case of that phenomenon of the Middle Ages to which
M. Guizot has drawn attention, the co-existence of two
opposing theories of law without any apparent percep-
tion of their discord in the minds of the men who had
to carry them into practice. But though both Charles

and the pope are spoken of as sovereigns in these
territories it appears probable—we cannot say more—
that Hadrian, had he been closely questioned on the
subject, would have recognised that even in the duchy of
Rome he was, in a manner difficult to define, subject to
the over-lordship of the Frankish king.

As has been said, the conduct of Charles in reference
to the kingdom of Italy, if that of an ambitious man,
was on the whole wise and statesmanlike. This praise
can hardly be given to his relations to the papacy, in
which there was a want of that clear and frank statement of what was granted and what was withheld, which
is the only means of avoiding future misunderstandings
between the giver and the receiver of a benefit. And
the consequences of this omission weighed heavily on
Europe for centuries, and often involved two really
upright and honest men, a Pope and an Emperor, in
hopeless quarrels.

If we may recur to the simile of a country parish
which was used in a foregoing chapter, the old absentee
squire and the big Nonconformist farmer have both
vanished from the scene. In their stead we have a new
squire, young, enthusiastic, and devoted to the Church,
who, as all the rustics see, is "hand and glove with the
parson." But he has other large estates in a distant
county which claim the greater portion of his time ; and,
partly in his haste to return to them, partly in the
effusion of his ecclesiastical zeal, he makes or is understood to make to his clerical friend such promises of
subscriptions, endowments, rebuildings, and upholdings
as he finds in after days of calmer calculation would
practically exhaust his whole rent-roll.

CHAPTER VI

THE CONVERSION OF THE SAXONS

THE year 772, which opened upon a reunited Frankish kingdom (Carloman having died at the close of the year preceding), and which was a blank as far as Frankish operations in Italy were concerned, was memorable as witnessing the beginning of that long struggle with Saxon independence and Saxon heathenism which was to occupy thirty-two central years in the life of Charles the Great.

Whether he entered upon this struggle with a light heart it is impossible for us to say. Many a time he thought it was ended, but found that he had only bent not broken the stubborn spirit of his foes, and assuredly it was with no light heart that he found himself, when past middle life and entering on his sixth decade, still obliged to resume his Sisyphean labour.

The different tribes which made up the loosely bound confederation of the Saxons occupied those territories reaching to the Elbe on the east, and nearly to the Rhine on the west, which now bear the names of Hanover, Brunswick, Oldenburg and Westphalia. This block of territory was divided in nearly equal parts between the three tribes of the Westphalians, the Angarians and the Eastphalians, the first and the last, as we should expect from their names, occupying the western and eastern and the Angarians (or Engern) the central portion. Then, beyond the Elbe, between the German Ocean and the Baltic was seated a fourth section of the Saxon people who bore the name of the Nord-albingians, and whose territory must have pretty nearly corresponded with the modern duchy of Holstein.

Thus the Saxons had no connection with the present kingdom of Saxony, though part of Prussian Saxony was probably within their borders. As Professor Freeman says in his *Historical Geography of Europe* (p. 207), "After the breaking up of the great Saxon duchy (1191), from most of the old Saxon lands the Saxon name may be looked on as having altogether passed away. The name of Saxony as a geographical expression clave to the Eastphalian remnant of the old duchy, and to Thuringia and the Slavonic conquests to the East." One might add, that by a curious coincidence, Hanover, the home of the old continental Saxons, was for 123 years (1714-1837) ruled by descendants of Alfred the Great who were kings of the Saxons over the sea.

These Saxon neighbours of the Franks are not to be thought of as mere savages. They had probably to some extent exchanged the nomad life of the shepherd for the more settled habits of the tiller of the ground. The old Germanic institution of the Folksthing as described by Tacitus, still apparently flourished among them. They had already been brought into a sort of loose connection with the Frankish kingdom, having at intervals paid a

yearly tribute of 500 cows to a Merovingian king and
an Arnulfing mayor of the palace.   There does not seem
any reason to suppose that at the time of the accession
of Charles they nourished any thought of deadly enmity
to their Frankish neighbours, or would have dreamed of
uniting their tribes in a well-organised invasion of the
prosperous Rhine-lands—in fact, throughout the struggle
which followed, the inability of the Saxons to combine
for the mere purpose of defence against impending
invasion is conspicuous and absurd.   But no doubt they
were lawless and disagreeable neighbours, often indulging in such raids as for centuries kept the Scottish
Border in turmoil, and above all the majority of them were
still heathens.   The missionaries who like Boniface had
crossed the sea from England to convert their German
kinsfolk had hitherto laboured chiefly among the
Frisians, but had also made some impression on the
mass of Saxon heathenism.   From the fierce wars which
Penda, the heathen King of Mercia, waged with Christian
Northumberland, we can imagine what suspicious rage
the success of these English missionaries would arouse
in the minds of the still heathen chiefs of the East and
Westphalians.

But, after all, it is probable that on the religious as
well as on the political question the attack came from
the Frankish side.   It was not so much because the
Saxons resented the presence of Christian missionaries
among them, as because Charles resented the fact of the
Saxons continuing in heathenism, that the Thirty Years'
War of the eighth century was resolved on.   Throughout his kingly and imperial career Charles took the
religious part of his duties seriously.   It was not for

nothing that he bore the title of *Christianissimus Rex*, not
for nothing that St. Augustine's famous treatise, *De
Civitate Dei*, was the favourite companion of his leisure.
In his interviews with Pope Hadrian at Rome the reform
of the Church's discipline was apparently the chief
subject of conversation; and in the thirty-three Ecclesiastical Councils which were held during his reign he
zealously co-operated with the churchmen towards the
same end.   To such a ruler it was intolerable that
tribes which were connected, however loosely, with his
kingdom should still profess a belief in the absurdities
of heathenism.   They must be persuaded, or, if per-
suasion failed, they must be forced, to become Christians.

At an assembly of the Frankish nation held at
Worms (July ? 772) Charles announced his purpose of
carrying war into the country of the Saxons, and in the
early summer he marched with a large army, accompanied by a multitude of bishops, abbots, and presbyters,
into the territory of the Angarii, the central tribe.   The
frontier fortress of Eresburg was taken, and the invaders
pressed on to the place where, in the midst of a sacred
grove, stood the celebrated Irminsul, a column fashioned
to imitate the great world - sustaining ash Yggdrasil,
which was the chief object of worship of the Saxon
tribes.   The idol was hewn down, the temple overthrown, the hoard of gold and silver ornaments
deposited there by generations of devout Saxons carried
off into Frank-land.   The work of destruction lasted
three days.   It chanced that there was a great scarcity of
water in the place where the Irminsul had stood.   The
army was parched with thirst, and perhaps began to be
stirred by superstitious fears that the drought was a

punishment for the destruction of the idol.   Suddenly, at noonday, while all the army was resting, there was a rush of water along a dry river bed.   All the army had enough to drink, and recognised with thanks the Divine approval of their destructive labours.   Charles after this marched to the banks of the Weser, held there with the Saxons a great palaver (to borrow a word from modern reports of similar conferences), and received their submission, for what it was worth, accompanied by the surrender of twelve hostages.

It would be tedious to copy the particulars, meagre as they are, given by the chroniclers concerning the eighteen campaigns in which Charles slowly and remorselessly beat down the resistance of the Saxons. It will be sufficient to notice some of the chief moments of the struggle.

In 774 Charles, intent on his operations in Italy, had left the Saxon March comparatively unguarded.   Seizing their opportunity, and apparently heedless of the fate of the twelve hostages who were in the hands of Charles, the heathen crossed the frontier in great force and entered Hesse, which they laid waste with fire and sword.   The objective of their attack was the abbey and church of Fritzlar, which had been founded near half a century before by the great Englishman, St. Boniface.   The saint had prophesied that his church should never be destroyed by fire, and the barbarians certainly seem to have been prevented—by supernatural means, says the legend—from wrapping it in flames, but there can be little doubt that they robbed it of all its treasures, thus taking speedy revenge for the destruction of their own Irminsul.   Charles meanwhile returned

from his triumphant campaign in Italy only to hear
of the insult that had been offered to his crown and his
creed by a barbarous foe. The season was far advanced,
but, mustering his troops at Ingelheim (a little south-
west of Mainz), he sent them in four squadrons into
Saxon-land. Three of the squadrons found the Saxons
and fought them; the fourth marched through their
land unopposed. All returned laden with booty to the
Rhine.

Charles spent the winter of 774-775 in his palace at
Quierzy, on the Oise, and there came to the conclusion
" that he would attack the perfidious and truce-breaking
nation of the Saxons in war, and would persevere therein
until they were either conquered and made subject to
the Christian religion or were altogether swept off the
face of the earth." It was easier to form a ruthless
resolution like this in the privacy of the palace
than to carry it into actual execution. The campaign
of 775, though planned on a large scale, does not differ
greatly from previous campaigns in character. The
king held a general assembly at Düren, at which
apparently the programme of "Christianity or death"
for the Saxons was submitted and approved. Then, in
August, Charles marched eastwards, took from the Westphalians their strong fortress of Sigiburg, on the Ruhr;
retook Eresburg, which had been taken by the Angarii;
and then pressed on into the land of the Eastphalians,
who do not appear to have offered any serious resistance
to his arms. But both with the Angarii and the Eastphalians the campaign ended with the usual formalities
of oaths of fealty and surrender of hostages; we do not
yet hear of that wholesale conversion or extirpation

which Charles had vowed at his setting forth. Moreover, while he was thus penetrating into the recesses of
the enemies' country, part of his force, which he had
left in Westphalia to guard his communications with the
Rhine, suffered a serious loss from a Saxon surprise.
Their camp was pitched at Lidbach, near Minden; it
was three o'clock in the afternoon; some of the cavalry
had gone forth to forage for their horses; the rest of
the army was indulging in a siesta; a troop of Saxons
mingled with the returning foragers, feigning themselves
to be their comrades (of course the warriors of that day
wore no uniform), and thus obtained admission to the
camp, where they made great slaughter of the half-
asleep and unarmed soldiers. It is said that the
Franks succeeded at last in driving the invaders out of
the camp, and that Charles, hurrying from the east, slew
a multitude of the retreating Saxons, but it is probable
that we have here the story, only slightly veiled, of a
serious Frankish reverse. Next year (776) Eresburg,
taken and retaken, was again the prize of war.
Sigiburg was attacked, but bravely and successfully
defended. Charles came with impetuous rush to the
sources of the Lippe, and found there a multitude of
Saxons, who had flocked thither from all quarters, and
who, terrified by Charles's successes, declared their
willingness to embrace Christianity, to become faithful
subjects of Charles and of the Franks, and to perform
the symbolical act by which they would give him corporal
possession of the soil of their country. An innumerable
multitude of Saxons, with their wives and children, were
baptized in the Lippe stream that flowed past the
Frankish camp; hostages, as many as Charles asked

for, were given; Eresburg was rebuilt, many other castles were reared, detachments of Franks were posted throughout the country, and the king returned into Frank-land to keep his Christmas at Heristal and his Easter at Nimeguen, feeling probably that the programme of Quierzy was now realised, and that the heathen and truce-breaking Saxons had at last become Christians and stable subjects of his realm.

But the subjugation was only apparent; there was one man ready, at least for a time, to play the part of Arminius, and to resist foreign domination to the death. The next nine years of the long contest (777-785) may be best characterised as the years of Widukind's strife for freedom.

In the year 777 King Charles held a public synod at Paderborn in the heart of Saxon-land. It was attended, not only by all the Frankish nobles, but also by nearly all the chiefs of the Saxon tribes. "Perfidiously," says the chronicler, "did they promise to mould their manners to the king's mind, and to devote themselves to his service. They received pardon from the king on this condition, that if thereafter they violated his statutes, they should be deprived of fatherland and freedom. At the same place there were baptized a very great multitude who, although falsely, had declared that they wished to become Christians."

But at this great assembly there was not seen the face of Widukind, a Westphalian chief who had large possessions both in Westphalia and also in Mid Saxony, and who must have already taken a leading part in the resistance to the Frankish arms, since he was, says the chronicler, "conscious of having committed many crimes and feared to face the king, wherefore he had fled to Sigfrid, King of the Danes."

Next year Charles led his army into Spain on that memorable expedition which ended in the disaster of Roncesvalles. Hearing that he was engaged in so remote a region, and perhaps also having some tidings of his ill-success, the Saxons, headed by Widukind, rose in rebellion, crossed the hills which formed their Western boundary and poured into the valley of the Rhine. The great river itself, not the Frankish armies, barred their further progress, but they rushed along the right bank from Deutz to Coblentz ravaging and burning. "Buildings sacred and profane were equally laid in ruins. No distinction of age or of sex was made by their hostile fury, so that it was plainly manifest that not for the sake of booty but in order to wreak vengeance they had crossed the frontier of the Franks." Incidentally we learn that so great was the terror caused by this inroad that the monks of Fulda took from the tomb their greatest treasure, the body of the holy Boniface, and journeyed with it two days into Frankish territory, but then hearing that the tide of invasion was turned, went back to redeposit their treasure at Fulda. For Charles, on learning the tidings of the Saxon invasion, had not thought it necessary with his war-wearied army to undertake a regular campaign, but had sent a flying squadron of Franks, who by forced marches came up with the Saxons at the river Eder, attacked them while crossing the stream, and inflicted upon them grievous loss.

In the next few years we hear the oft-repeated story of rapid marches right through Saxon-land even to the Elbe, no effectual stand made by the Saxons, but raids and insurrections headed by the restless Widukind.   In 780 Charles begins to busy himself with the ecclesiastical organisation of the conquered country.   In 782 (apparently) he holds a *placitum* at the sources of the Lippe, and there promulgates his stern *Capitulatio de partibus Saxoniae*.   On any one who violently enters a church and robs it, shall be inflicted the punishment of death; on any one who despises the Christian custom of Lent and eats flesh therein, death (but his life may be saved if the priest shall certify that flesh was necessary for his health); on any one who slays bishop or presbyter, death; on any one who in pagan fashion believes in witchcraft and burns the supposed witch, death; on any one practising cremation instead of burial, death; on any Saxon hiding himself in order to escape baptism and remain in paganism, death; on any one offering sacrifice to the demons of the pagans, death; on any one who shall conspire with the pagans against the Christians, or seek to continue with them in hostility to the Christian faith, death.   Yet if, after privily committing any of these crimes, the criminal shall flee to a priest, make confession and do penance, on the priest's testimony the capital punishment shall be remitted.   At the same time a strict tithe-law was passed.   "We enact that according to the command of God, all men, whether nobles, freeborn men or *liti* (serfs), shall give the tenth part of their substance and labour to the churches and priests, so that as God shall have given to every Christian he shall restore a part to God."

This rigorous Act of Uniformity stirred the deep resentment of the Saxons.   But perhaps discontent might not have burst into a flame but for the return of

Widukind from his wonted Danish refuge, and for the harangues with which he stirred the vain hopes of the Saxons and roused them to revolt (782). At the same time tidings were brought to Charles of an incursion of a Sclavonic tribe, the Sorabi, from beyond the Elbe. The Frankish king presumed too far on the apparent pacification of Saxon-land. Like his great imitator, Napoleon, he would use the last-conquered people to subdue the enemy next beyond them, and he sent an army composed of Saxons as well as Austrasian Franks to repel the Sclavonic incursion. Adalgisus the chamberlain, Geilo the count of the stables, and Worad the count of the palace, commanded the motley host; but when they entered Saxon-land they found the whole country already in a flame, and the Saxons, by the advice of Widukind, about to march into Francia. Wisely postponing the expedition against the Sorabi, they marched with their Frankish troops—the Saxon contingent had doubtless deserted—to the place where they heard that the rebel host was gathered. In the heart of the enemies' country they met Count Theodoric, a relation of the king's, who had made a hasty levy of troops in Rhine-land on hearing of the Saxon revolt. Seeing the over-zeal of the three courtiers, Theodoric advised them to make careful reconnaissances of the enemy's position, and proposed that, if the ground proved favourable, a joint attack should be made on the Saxon camp at the hill Suntal, near Minden. In pursuance of the suggested plan, they crossed the Weser and pitched their camp on the north bank of the river. Then, fearing that the renown of the joint victory would accrue to the king's cousin Theodoric, they determined to attack the Saxons alone. Underrating the steadfastness of their foes they dashed headlong and in loose order into the camp, more as if they were pursuing a flying foe than charging an enemy drawn up in order of battle. This time the Frankish fury failed before the stolid Saxon stubbornness. They were surrounded by the enemy, and terrible slaughter was made in their ranks. A few Franks escaped, not to their quarters of the morning, but to the camp of Theodoric ; but Adalgisus and Geilo, four counts, twenty nobles of high rank, and a multitude of followers, who, in the true spirit of the old German *comitatus*, preferred to die rather than survive their lords, fell on the field of fight. The battle of Mount Suntal was certainly the greatest disaster that befell the Frankish arms in the whole course of the Thirty Years' War.

Terrible was the anger of Charles when he heard of the Saxon rising, of the murders of priests and monks with which it had been accompanied, and lastly of the deep humiliation inflicted on his race by the defeat of the three generals. He collected a large army and entered the land of the Saxons. When thus in earnest he seems to have been always able to crush their resistance. Widukind fled for the fourth or fifth time to Denmark, and the land lay prostrate at the feet of Charles. He summoned before him all the chiefs of the Saxons, and made inquisition concerning the author of the revolt. With one voice all named Widukind, the absent Widukind. As he could not be arrested, the men who had listened to his persuasions must suffer. Four thousand five hundred men (including probably some of the chiefs of the nation) who had shown themselves foremost in the revolt were surrendered to Charles.

It was expected probably that the ringleaders only out of this number would suffer; but Charles was evidently in a Berserk rage. All the 4500 Saxons were beheaded in one day at Verden on the banks of the Aller. "Having perpetrated this act of vengeance, the king went into winter quarters at the villa of Theodo, and there celebrated the birth of our Lord, and there also the festival of Easter, according to his wonted custom."

The year 783 was to Charles a year of domestic sorrow but of military triumph. His wife Hildegard (whom he had married immediately after the repudiation of the daughter of Desiderius) died on the 30th of April; his loved and honoured mother, Bertrada, on the 12th of July; but immediately after his wife's funeral he entered Saxon-land with a powerful army, vanquished his enemies with great slaughter at Detmold, vanquished them again in the neighbourhood of Osnabrück, where "there was slain of the Saxons an infinite multitude, great booty was taken, and a large number of captives was led away." He then swept with his victorious army from the Weser to the Elbe, ravaging wherever he went—for it was thus that this great preacher of Christianity argued for the faith—and then returning to Frank-land married his fourth wife, Fastrada, the daughter of the Frankish count Radolf.

The next year (784) was somewhat less successful, owing to widespread inundations, the result of sudden and heavy rains, which stopped the victor's progress northward; but his young son Charles, who had been left with a part of the army in Westphalia while Charles himself went southward towards Thuringia, won a great cavalry battle on the banks of the Lippe. And this

year Charles made a new departure. After a short
autumnal visit to Frank-land, he returned into Saxon-
land, spent his Christmas in the neighbourhood of
Pyrmont, and went into winter quarters at the now
strongly fortified Eresburg.

"And when he had decided to winter there," says the
chronicler, "having sent for wife and children to join
him, and having left in the said camp a sufficiently
staunch and strong garrison, he went forth himself with
a flying squadron to lay waste the townships of the
Saxons and to plunder their farms, and thus by
himself and by the generals whom he sent in different
directions, marching everywhere, and everywhere carrying
fire and slaughter, he paid back the Saxons in their own
coin and gave them a sufficiently uneasy winter." After
holding a general assembly at Paderborn, Charles
marched unopposed through Saxon-land as far as the
Elbe. In the district of Bardengau, near the mouth of
that river, Charles halted, looking across the river to the
territory of the yet unsubdued Transalbian Saxons who
dwelt in the land that is now called Holstein. While he
was here news was brought to him that Widukind and a
confederate, perhaps a kinsman, named Abbio were
willing to surrender themselves and forswear further
resistance if they could be assured of their personal
safety. A Frankish courtier named Amalwin was sent
across the Elbe with hostages for the safe-conduct which
he bore to the two Saxon chiefs. They accompanied him
on his return, and were brought into the presence of
Charles, who was by this time back again across the
Rhine and at his palace of Attigny on the Aisne, near
the forest of Ardennes. Charles received his fallen foes

graciously. They were both baptized, Charles himself acting as godfather to Widukind and presenting him with costly gifts. As far as we can see, both honestly accepted the duties which the pledge of fealty to the most Christian king involved. Authentic history after this point is silent as to the name of Widukind, but legends, for which there is very likely some foundation, represent him as not only a contented but even an ardent votary of his new faith, a founder of churches and convents, and an endower of the bishopric of Minden. It is probable that he was allowed to retain his large possessions in Westphalia, and he has been chosen as a favourite peg by German genealogists on which to hang the descent of their Serene and Princely patrons. The least doubtful of these pedigrees appears to be that which makes the great Emperor Otho a descendant, through his mother Matilda, of the Saxon hero.

The submission of Widukind ended for the time the resistance of the Saxons. "That obstinacy of the Saxon perfidy rested for some years, chiefly for this reason, that they could not find opportunities for revolting suitable to the matter in hand," is the quaint remark of the chronicler.

This peace lasted for six or seven years, in one of which (789) we are told that the king "arranged all matters pertaining to the Saxons, suitably to the time." That is to say, no doubt, the yoke of Church and State was being fitted to the stubborn Saxon neck. So confident was Charles of the subjugation of his foe that he employed both Saxons and Frisians in the campaigns in which he was now busily engaged on the Middle Danube against the kingdom of the Avars.

The fact, however, that the Frankish power was thus
engaged in a tough struggle with an enemy in the south,
at last emboldened the Saxons to make another stand
for freedom.   Again they allied themselves with the
Frisians, and on the 6th of July 792 the first blow was
struck.   A portion of Charles's army which had, for
some unexplained purpose, been sent in ships to the
mouth of the Elbe was set upon by the insurgents of the
two allied nations and cut to pieces.   This evidence of
unslumbering hostility does not seem to have effectually
diverted Charles's attention from his Danubian campaign,
but next year (793) tidings of a similar but more over-
whelming disaster were brought to him at his quarters
in Bavaria.   Count Theodoric, the king's kinsman and a
valiant and trusted general (the same who had saved
the Frankish army from annihilation on the disastrous
day of Suntal), had been leading an army through the
district of Rustringen, on the borders of Friesland and
Saxon-land, and at some little distance to the west of
the Weser.   The reason for his presence in that region is
not told us, but it was probably the desire to check the
revolt which had burst forth in the preceding summer.
What is certain is that he was set upon by the Saxons,
his army destroyed, and apparently himself slain.   Now,
at any rate, if not already in the previous year, the
rebellion assumed that character of ruthless vindictive-
ness, especially against churchmen, which showed how
sorely the Saxons had been galled by Charles's ecclesiastical ordinances.   "As a dog returneth to his vomit,"
says an annalist, "so did they return to the paganism
which they had aforetime renounced, again deserting
Christianity, lying not less to God than to their lord the

king, who had conferred upon them so many benefits,
and joining themselves to the pagan nations who dwelt
round about them. Sending their emissaries to the
Avars, they endeavoured to rebel first against God, then
against the king and the Christians. They laid waste
all the churches which were within their borders with
burning and destruction; they rejected the bishops and
presbyters who were set over them; some they took
prisoners and others they slew, and, in short, they turned
themselves right round to the worship of idols."

When the news of Theodoric's defeat reached the
king it found him, as before stated, in camp in the
centre of Bavaria. The war with the Avars was pros-
pering, but it was still a long way from completion. To
deal with two enemies in such widely separated regions
as Hanover and Hungary was a hard problem for a
commander-in-chief in the eighth century. Charles sought
to solve it by a characteristic stroke of his truly imperial
genius, and though he failed, even the failure attests the
grandeur of his conceptions. Near the Bavarian town of
Weissenburg a little stream called the Schwäbische
Rezat takes its rise, within a few miles of a larger river,
the Altmühl. The Rezat flows northward into the
Main, and so eventually into the Rhine and the German
Ocean. The Altmühl, on the other hand, soon reaches
the Danube, and so sends its waters at last into the
Black Sea. Charles's idea (suggested to him by some
professed experts, but eagerly embraced) was to make a
navigable canal between the Rezat and the Altmühl,
and thus transport his troops and their provisions at
will by river navigation either northward against the
Saxons or eastward against the Avars. During the

whole autumn of 793 a vast multitude of men laboured
at the great enterprise. They dug a fosse two miles
long and three hundred feet wide, but it was all in vain.
Nature was too strong for them. The marshy quality
of the soil, made worse by autumnal rains, thwarted the
operations of the diggers, and however much they dug
out by day, by night the heaps had all sunk back into
the swampy level. There is still, however, a trench
about five miles south-west of Weissenburg called the
Fossa Carolina, which remains as a monument of the great
king's project. " What a change " (as has been truly
said by Pastor Meier, a Bavarian priest who traced the
course of the Roman *Limes Imperii* through these
regions), " what stir, and what activity would have
filled all those quiet plains if the grand scheme of
Kaiser Karl [not yet Kaiser] had been realised, and this
tiny streamlet, the Rezat, had seen the interchange of
the products of the east and west." The scheme itself,
or something like it, was carried into execution by King
Louis I. of Bavaria, but owing to the introduction of the
railway system König-Ludwigs-Kanal, like so many
other artificial waterways, has lost much of its importance.

Foiled in this endeavour King Charles allowed the
year 793 to pass without an attempt to punish the
Saxon rebellion. The next six years (794-799) each
had its Saxon campaign. The general features of the
war are very similar to those which we have already
noticed : rapid marches of the Frankish king, devastation of the Saxon country, oaths of submission and
Saxon hostages. It is noteworthy that Charles now
carries back into Frank-land large numbers of these
hostages—all apparently young lads—has them educated

as Christians, generally as ecclesiastics, and when peace is restored instals them in the various churches and convents wherewith, as the Roman *imperator* of old with his *coloniæ*, he fastens down the conquered country. It is also to be observed that the struggle is now chiefly confined to the northern part of Saxon-land, to the great *gau* of Wigmodia, which stretched between Bremen and Hamburg, and to the Nordalbingi who, as has been said, occupied what is now the duchy of Holstein. Further, that Charles, Teuton as he was, did not object to avail himself of the help of a Sclavonic people, the Abodrites, who were the eastern neighbours of the Saxons, and that he bitterly avenged the death of their king Witzin on "the perfidious Saxon nation," into whose snares he had fallen (795).

In several of these campaigns the Frankish king was effectually seconded by his son Charles, now a young man of between twenty and thirty, to whom it was the father's custom to entrust a portion of his army that a combined attack might be made from different points of the compass. The plan of operations seems to have been generally well laid, for we never hear of these concerted invasions failing to meet at the point agreed upon.

One of the fiercest campaigns was that of 798 against the Nordalbingi, who had grievously enraged Charles by the murder of his *missi* or plenipotentiaries, one of whom was clothed with the sacred character of an ambassador to the King of Denmark. In his vengeance for this murder Charles was powerfully seconded by Thrasco, Duke of the Abodrites.

During the next four eventful years (800-803) Charles

had abundant occupation south of the Alps. In 804 he led his army into Saxon-land, "transferred all the Saxons who dwelt beyond the Elbe and in Wigmodia with their wives and children into Frank-land, and gave the shires beyond the Elbe to the Abodrites." As these Sclavonian allies of Charles were heathens, this handing over to them of the duchy of Holstein was so far a confession of failure in the attempt to win the whole of the Saxon territory for Christianity. The number of the Saxons on both banks of the Elbe thus transported is given by Einhard at 10,000. When the inhabitants of whole districts were thus forcibly removed, much injustice, even from the point of view of Frankish "law and order," must often have been committed. In the next generation complaints reached the ears of Charles's successor from the sons of loyal and peaceable dwellers by the Weser who had been swept off into exile together with the rebel Wigmodians, and had never recovered the property of which they were then despoiled.

The resistance of the Saxons was powerfully aided by their Danish neighbour on the north. "Godofrid, King of Denmark," says the chronicler, "with his fleet and all the cavalry of his kingdom came to a place which is called Sliesthorp, on the borders of his kingdom and Saxon-land, for a conference with Charles, but would not venture further. Charles remained close to the river Elbe in a place which is called Holdunsteti, from whence he sent an embassy to Godofrid to treat about the surrender of deserters." As "the place called Sliesthorp" is Schleswig, and "the place called Holdunsteti" is Holstein, the student of contemporary history will recognise in this passage the germs of that controversy on "the Schleswig-Holstein question" which was settled in our day by the Dano-German war and led eventually to the supremacy of Prussia in the Germanic Confederation.

At last the Saxon war was ended. The wholesale transportation of inhabitants to which Charles had at length resorted, and which was balanced by the invitation to Franks to settle in the evacuated lands—acts which remind us of the proceedings of Shalmaneser and Nebuchadnezzar towards the people of Israel—had the desired effect.

> "Freedom's battle once begun
> Bequeathed from bleeding sire to son"

in this instance was not "ever won." Christianity, or a religion which believed itself to be Christianity, was triumphant from the Rhine to the Elbe, and three fat bishoprics, Bremen, Münster, and Paderborn, divided between themselves the conquered land. "Saxonia" was henceforth an inseparable part of the newly-founded Frankish Empire.

CHAPTER VII

REVOLTS AND CONSPIRACIES

In tracing the history of Charles's long struggle with
the Saxons we have come down to a very late point in
the story of his reign. We must now retrace our steps
and notice some of the more important events that happened during that struggle of thirty years. And first
it will be well to deal with some of the unsuccessful
attempts that were made in various parts of his
dominions, other than Saxon-land, to throw off the yoke
of this strong and masterful ruler.

Less than two years after the downfall of the Lombard monarchy, at the end of 775, when Charles was
fully committed to his life-and-death contest with
Saxon heathenism, he received tidings of an attempt on
the part of at least one Lombard duchy to recover its
independence. Before leaving Italy he had either
appointed a Lombard noble named Hrodgaud, Duke of
Friuli, or had confirmed him in the possession of that
duchy. Forum Julii, which we now know by the name
of Friuli, and whose chief city is now called Cividale,
included the fertile lands north of the Venetian Gulf,
and was of primary importance to the Frankish king as

it touched on the one side the provinces of Venetia and Istria (wavering at this time between allegiance to him and their old allegiance to Constantinople) and on the other side the lands of the Duke of Bavaria, who, as we shall soon see, was one of the most untrustworthy of subject princes.

Hrodgaud appears to have been engaged in some obscure negotiations with the Lombard dukes of Chiusi and Benevento for cutting short the new papal territories, perhaps also for bringing in the exiled son of Desiderius and raising once more the standard of Lombard independence. But the combination failed, owing perhaps in part to the death of the Emperor Constantine V., which happened in the autumn of 775. The young Lombard prince Adelchis failed to make his appearance in Italy; the Dukes of Chiusi and Benevento hung back from the dangerous enterprise and Hrodgaud of Friuli was left alone to meet the Frankish avenger. His courage did not fail; he seems to have proclaimed himself king, doubtless "King of the Lombards," and persuaded many cities in Northern Italy to join his standard. But Charles, warned of his revolt before the end of 775, crossed the Alps in the early months of 776. The passes cannot yet have been open, and it must have been with a small but select body of troops that he made his rapid descent upon Friuli. Hrodgaud seems to have fallen in battle. Cividale surrendered. Treviso, where Hrodgaud's father-in-law, Stabilinus, sought to prolong the struggle, was also captured and was the scene of Charles's Easter festivities. All the other revolted cities were taken, and in June Charles recrossed the Alps to march swiftly northward to recapture the oft-taken Eresburg, and to baptize some thousands of Saxons in the Lippe.

Considering the difficulties of locomotion at that time this short Italian campaign against Hrodgaud seems to have been one of the most rapid and brilliant of all the military operations of King Charles. The suppression of the revolt was followed, not indeed by bloodshed, but by severe confiscations of the property of the insurgents. We have a piteous account by the great Lombard historian, Paulus Diaconus, of the seven years' captivity of his brother, who is generally believed to have been punished for his share in this insurrection. " My brother languishes a captive in your land, broken-hearted, in nakedness and want. His unhappy wife, with quivering lips, begs for bread from street to street. Four children must she support in this humiliating manner, whom she is scarce able to cover even with rags."

The next threatening of internal disaffection came from a quarter in which the sky had long looked lower-ing. Tassilo III., Duke of Bavaria, was the most inde-pendent and high-spirited of all the subject nobles in the Frankish kingdom. Sprung from the old Agilolfing line, which for more than two centuries had ruled the Bavarian people, he had some pretensions to a descent from Merovingian royalty, and was the undoubted grandson of Charles Martel, and therefore first cousin of King Charles, with whom he was strictly contemporary, having been born in the year 742. The dependence of Bavaria upon the Frankish crown had always been of the slightest kind, consisting of little more than a verbal recognition of the supremacy of the Frankish king, and the sending of a contingent to serve in the Frankish army, while, in all the details of ordinary administration, the will of the Agilolfing duke seems to have been practically supreme. Moreover, close ties of affinity and common interests had long united the ducal house of Bavaria and the regal house of Lombard Italy. Together they had resisted the incursions of their turbulent neighbours on the east, the Avars and the Sclaves; together they had sought, rather by diplomacy than by war, to keep at a distance from them the domineering Frank.

In the later years of Pippin, as has been already stated, this tendency of Bavaria to independence was openly displayed. It is true that in the year 757, when Pippin was holding his *placitum* at Compiègne, thither came the young Tassilo with the chiefs of his nation, and, "after the Frankish manner placing his hands in the hands of the king, commended himself unto him in vassalage, and promised fidelity both to King Pippin himself and to his sons Charles and Carloman by an oath on the body of St. Dionysius, and not only there, but also over the bodies of St. Martin and St. Germanus with a similar oath promised that he would keep faith towards his aforesaid lords all the days of his life. And similarly all the chiefs and seniors of the Bavarians who had come with him into the presence of the king promised at the said holy places that they would keep faith towards the king and his sons." But the very insistence on this ceremony probably showed that the loyalty of the Bavarians was deemed precarious. It is certain that six years later (763), in the very crisis of the war with Aquitaine, "Tassilo, Duke of Bavaria, neglected his oaths and all his promises, forgot all the benefits which he had received from his uncle, King Pippin, and, making a fraudulent excuse of sickness, withdrew himself from the campaign. Then, strengthening his resolution to revolt, he stoutly declared that he would come no more into the king's presence." This was nothing less than to commit the crime of *harisliz* (military desertion), which, according to Frankish law, was punishable by death. But as we saw, King Pippin wisely determined to fight with one enemy at a time, and devoted all his energies to the long war with Waifar of Aquitaine, a war which practically occupied him till the end of his days. Thus the *harisliz* of Tassilo III. went for the time unpunished.

Then came Charles's accession to the throne, and his marriage with the daughter of Desiderius. By this marriage a tie of affinity was formed between the two cousins, — the lord and the contumacious vassal, — for Tassilo also about the same time married another daughter of Desiderius, named Liutberga. It seemed for a short time as if Frank, Bavarian, and Lombard might dwell together in amity ; but only for a short time. Soon followed the repudiation of the Lombard princess, Pope Hadrian's cry for help, the invasion of Italy, the fall of the Lombard kingdom. During all these stirring events Tassilo seems to have remained quiescent, yet assuredly then, if ever, would have been his chance to assert the independence after which he yearned.

So too during the rebellion of Hrodgaud of Friuli, when doubtless he might have intercepted Charles's passage, and made the suppression of that rebellion a much more tedious affair than it actually was, Tassilo made no sign. He seems to have thought his sulky

attitude of isolation and *de facto* independence of his lord
would maintain itself without any trouble on his part,
but he was greatly mistaken. His Frankish over-lord
was no *roi fainéant* to let his rights thus quietly glide
into desuetude.

Charles tried first spiritual means, which were perhaps
suggested by the fact of his finding himself in the
presence of the pope. Towards the end of 780, in one
of those short lulls in the storm which made him deem
the work of the subjugation of the Saxons complete,
Charles visited Italy, kept his Christmas in the old
Lombard palace at Pavia, held a *placitum* at Mantua, and
at Easter visited Rome. He was accompanied by his
wife and his sons, Carloman and Louis, children of four
and three years old. Carloman, who had not yet been
baptized, was raised from the baptismal font by Pope
Hadrian, who gave him the ancestral name of Pippin,
and being anointed by the pope was declared by his
father to be King of Italy. At the same time his yet
more infantile brother, Louis, was anointed King of
Aquitaine. Of course in both cases all kingly power
remained in the hands of the great War-lord; but
apparently the object of the ceremony was something
like that which caused our Edward I. to name the baby
Edward of Caernarvon, Prince of Wales. National pride
was soothed, and national patriotism in some degree
reassured, by the presence of a court and the assurance
of a separate administration, even though the nominal
head of the court was a little child in the nursery.

While Charles was at Rome there was converse
between him and the pope concerning the Duke of
Bavaria. Tassilo had been a liberal friend to the

Church, and had successfully prosecuted the enterprise
of the conversion of the Sclaves on his eastern frontier.
Hadrian well knew how strained were the relations
between duke and king, and was, we may believe,
sincerely anxious to reconcile Tassilo to his mighty
cousin. A joint embassy was despatched to the Bavarian
court: the pope being represented by the bishops,
Damasus and Formosus, the king by the deacon Richulf
and Eberhard the arch-cupbearer. "And when," says
the chronicler, "these emissaries, obedient to their in-
struction, had conversed with the aforesaid duke, and
reminded him of his old oaths to King Pippin, King
Charles and the Franks, his heart was so much softened
that he declared his willingness to hasten at once to the
king's presence, if such hostages were given him as to
remove all doubt of his personal safety. These having
been given, he came without delay to the king at
Worms, swore the oath which was dictated to him, and
gave twelve chosen hostages for the fulfilment of his
promise that he would keep as towards King Charles
and his loyal subjects all the oaths which he had sworn
aforetime to King Pippin. These hostages were
promptly brought to the king in his villa of Quierzy by
Sindbert, Bishop of Ratisbon. But the said duke returning home did not long remain in the faith which he
had promised."

Notwithstanding the ominous words with which the
chronicler concludes, a great moral victory had certainly
been gained by Charles, and the attitude of sullen semi-
independence which Tassilo had maintained for nearly
twenty years was now abandoned.

For six years (781-787) the name of Tassilo disappears

from the chronicles, and we may conclude that he was for so long a fairly loyal subject of the Frankish kingdom, or rather perhaps that he committed no such open act of rebellion as to compel Charles, engrossed as he was during these years by the war with Widukind, to send any of his sorely needed Frankish warriors for the chastisement of his Bavarian vassal.

Moreover, the open enmity of the Saxons was not the only danger that at this time menaced the security of the Frankish throne. In the year 785, immediately after the baptism of Widukind, we have the following mysterious entry in the chronicles : "There was made in that same year on the other side of the Rhine a vast conspiracy of the eastern Franks against the king, of which it was proved that Count Hardrad was the author. But information thereof was speedily brought to the king, and by his shrewdness so mighty a conspiracy shortly collapsed without any great danger, the authors thereof being condemned, some to death, some to privation of sight, and some to deportation and exile." Even the king's life was aimed at by the conspirators, yet Einhard assures us that none of the conspirators were actually killed save three who drew their swords upon the officers who were sent to arrest them. The cause of this sudden outbreak of Austrasian jealousy and rage against the great Austrasian hero must remain a mystery. Some of the authorities seem to speak of it as a specially Thuringian conspiracy, and one attributes it to the refusal of a Thuringian chief to hand over his daughter to a Frankish suitor to whom she was betrothed. An attempt has been made to account for it as the last struggle of Thuringian independence, dismayed at seeing the Saxons

on the north and the Bavarians on the south subjected
to the all-mastering Frankish king. It seems, however,
more probable that it was a personal, palace conspiracy.
Possibly Einhard gives us the requisite clue when he
attributes both this and a subsequent conspiracy to the
cruelty of Charles's queen Fastrada who "diverted her
husband from the kindness and accustomed gentleness
of his nature."

Towards the end of 786 Charles again marched into
Italy, where the not only independent but even hostile
attitude of Arichis, Prince of Benevento, called for his
attention. Having spent his Christmas at Florence, and
paid his devotions at the tombs of the Apostles in Rome,
he proceeded southward (787), and on the confines of
the Beneventan territory was met by Romwald, son of
Arichis, with gifts and promises and entreaties that he
would not enter his father's territory. But Charles,
says the chronicler, "thinking that he must deal very
differently with an enterprise once begun, kept Romwald
with him and marched with all his army to Capua, where
he pitched his camp, and would have carried on the war
from thence, unless the aforesaid duke had anticipated
his intention by wholesome counsel. For leaving his
capital, Benevento, he betook himself with all his
followers to the seaport of Salerno, as being a more
fortified city, and, sending an embassy, he offered both
his sons to the king, promising that he would willingly
obey all his commands. Listening to these prayers, and
moved also by the fear of God, the king abstained from
war; and keeping the younger son Grimwald as a
hostage, sent the elder son back to his father. He,
moreover, received eleven hostages from the rest of the

nation, and sent ambassadors to strengthen the covenant
of the prince and all the people of Benevento by oaths."
Thus had the Frankish king, without striking a blow,
extended his dominion to the southernmost corner of
Italy. It was, however, a precarious conquest; and the
princes of Benevento were almost to the end of Charles's
reign either doubtful vassals or open enemies of the
Frankish ruler.

Easter of 787 was spent by King Charles in Rome,
and this visit, like that of five years before, was followed
by a further development of the contest between him
and Duke Tassilo.   Doubtless the hollow reconciliation
of 782 had been followed by mutual suspicion and
estrangement : and the Bavarian duke must have felt
that, with the Saxon rebellion now apparently quelled,
his turn for subjugation would come next.   While the
king was still in Rome, there appeared in that city two
Bavarian envoys, Arno Bishop of Salzburg, and Huneric
Abbot of Mond See, who besought the pope to mediate
between Charles and their master.   The pope, as before,
expressed his hearty goodwill towards Tassilo, and an
interview between king and envoys followed in his
presence.   But when Charles called upon the bishop
and the abbot to state what guarantee their master had
empowered them to give for the fulfilment, this time, of
his often violated promises, they could only answer that
they had no instructions on this head, being not plenipotentiaries on Tassilo's behalf, only messengers whose
duty it was to carry back to their master the propositions
of the king and pontiff.   Apparently, then, the duke had
reverted to that old position of all but equality with the
Frankish king which he took up twenty-four years

before at the time of the great *harisliz*, and the solemnly
plighted oaths sworn at Worms were to go for nothing.
Hadrian was not less indignant than Charles at this
exhibition of fickleness and bad faith, and appears to
have visited his displeasure on the two churchmen-
ambassadors themselves, telling them that they and
their master were all liars together, and that they should
all be visited by the papal anathema unless Tassilo kept
the oaths which he had sworn to Charles and to Pippin.
We have here one of the earliest instances of that use
of ecclesiastical censures to enforce political claims which
was so characteristic a feature of the Middle Ages.

The ambassadors returned to Bavaria empty-handed :
and the king, recrossing the Alps, went to rejoin his
wife, the hard and haughty Fastrada, at Worms.   Probably her influence was not used to soften his temper
towards the rebellious duke.   A general assembly was
called, to which the king rehearsed all the events of his
Italian journey, concluding with the story of the abortive
negotiations with Tassilo.   By the advice probably of
his nobles, one more embassy was sent to claim from the
Bavarian the fulfilment of his promises and to summon
him to the royal presence.   On his refusal, Frankish invaders from three different points entered the devoted
duchy.   Italian Pippin from the South marched from
Trient up the valley of the Adige and over the water-
shed of the Inn ; Charles himself crossed the Lech and
entered Bavaria from the west by way of Augsburg.
A little further to the north, near Ingoldstadt, came an
army of Austrasian Franks, including not only Thuringians but even Saxons, so great was Charles's confidence
in that pacification of the country which, as after events

showed, was then but half completed. Seeing himself
thus surrounded, and also knowing that many of his own
subjects would side with the invaders—for apparently
to the ordinary Bavarian landowner the prospect of a
distant lord paramount at Aachen or Quierzy was more
acceptable than the reality of a present and stringent
master on the banks of the Danube—Tassilo gave up
the game, presented himself at Charles's headquarters,
handed over to him a stick, carved into some resemblance of a man, as a symbol of the land for which
he did homage, and gave as a hostage his son Theodo,
who for the last ten years had been associated with him
as ruler of the duchy. Hostages, as usual, twelve in
number, were given for Tassilo's adherence to his freshly
made promises, and at the same time the people of the
land were in some way, the details of which are not dis-
closed, made parties to his oath of fidelity to Charles.

It is not easy to account for the harsh proceedings of
the next year (788) after this apparent reconciliation of
the vassal to his lord. Possibly something had come to
light which justified Charles in the belief that Tassilo
would never honestly accept the position of vassal from
which he had so often endeavoured to escape. An
assembly was convened at Ingelheim, probably in the
month of June. Tassilo, now helpless and unarmed,
was summoned to appear before it, and was there
accused, on the evidence of some of his own subjects
who were loyal to Charles, of having opened negotiations with the barbarous Avars on the east after his
last submission to the Frankish king. Liutberga, his
Lombard queen, mindful of the old feud and of her
father's wrongs, was said to have been the ceaseless

preacher of revenge. Even against the life of Charles,
Tassilo was accused of having conspired, and when men
spoke to him of the danger in which he thus placed
his hostage-son, he is said to have answered : " Had I
ten sons I would lose them all in this cause, since it
were better for me to die than to live a vassal on such
ignominious terms as I have sworn to." Then the old
accusation of the *harisliz* of 763 was brought up against
him, and on this and other charges he was found guilty
by the assembled nobles, Franks, and Bavarians,
Lombards and Saxons, assembled from all parts of
Charles's realm, and by their united voice was adjudged
worthy of death.   This sentence, however, was commuted
by "the most pious Charles, moved by compassion and
the love of God and because he was his kinsman : and he
obtained from his own servants and the servants of God
[the nobles secular and religious] this favour, that he
should not die. Then Tassilo, being asked by the most
clement king what he wished, begged that he might have
leave to assume the tonsure and enter a monastery,
there to do penance for so many sins, that he might
save his soul.   Similarly his son Theodo was sentenced,
tonsured, and sent into a monastery, and the few
Bavarians who chose to remain in opposition to King
Charles were banished."

According to one authority, Tassilo, while accepting
tranquilly the decree which consigned him for the rest
of his days to the monotonous seclusion of a convent,
begged that his long hair, the symbol of his Frankish or
even Merovingian descent, might not be shorn off in
public, in the sight of his Frankish compeers, his
Bavarian followers and companions in arms, and this

favour was granted him by the clemency of the king. He was sent at once to the monastery of St. Goar on the Rhine, and afterwards to the safer seclusion of Jumièges in Normandy. His sons and his daughters were also persuaded or compelled to enter various convents: his wife, scion of that unhappy race which seemed doomed to disaster in all its members, was either banished or like the rest of her family accepted the sentence of seclusion in the cloister. Once more does Tassilo appear upon the stage of history, when in the year 794 he was brought to the assembly at Frankfort (an assembly convened ostensibly for a purely theological purpose) and there "made his peace with the lord the king, renouncing all the power which he had once held in Bavaria and handing it over to the king." It is suggested that the law had been somewhat strained by Tassilo's condemnation in the assembly at Ingelheim and that this formal and professedly voluntary surrender of his rights was deemed necessary to perfect Charles's title as ruler of Bavaria. After this event Tassilo vanishes from the scene, the year and place of his death being alike unrecorded by authentic history.

For the later history of Europe and especially of Germany, the deposition of Tassilo and the vindication of the imperilled Frankish supremacy over Bavaria were perhaps even·more important than the perpetually recurring Saxon campaigns which fill so large a space in Charles's annals. Sooner or later Saxon-land was almost certain to become Christian and civilised, and so to enter the Frankish orbit: but at Charles's accession there seemed to be a great probability that Bavaria would turn her *de facto* independence into

separation *de jure* from the Frankish realm. This would
have caused a separation of the Germany of the future
into two independent states, a kingdom of the North
and a kingdom of the South, which, as we know, never
actually took place in the Middle Ages.

With one more conspiracy, this time of a domestic
character, the tale of treasons is ended. In the year
792 (the year in which Charles had an Avar war and a
Saxon rebellion on his hands at once, and made his
abortive attempt to join the Danube and the Rhine by
a canal), there was added to all his other cares a rebellion
headed by one of his own flesh and blood. His eldest
son Pippin was apparently not born in wedlock, though
his mother Himiltrud, after her son's birth, probably
became Charles's lawfully wedded wife. This defect of
legitimacy would not have been an insuperable bar to
succession in a house which derived its chief glories from
the illegitimate Charles Martel; but there was another
and more fatal circumstance in the case of Charles's
firstborn. Though beautiful in face he was deformed,
probably dwarfish in figure, an unsuitable person therefore to be presented to the assembled Frankish warriors
as heir to his father's kingdom. Thus Pippin, though
to a certain extent maintaining his princely rank, and
named next to his father in the litanies of the Church,
seems to have been silently edged out from all hope
of succeeding to any portion of that father's power.
Charles, the eldest son of Hildegard, was apparently
recognised as principal heir. Carloman and Louis were
taken to Rome in their infancy and anointed Kings of
Italy and Aquitaine, while Pippin was left unnoticed.
Perhaps even the imposition of the ancestral name of

Pippin on the child Carloman was meant as a hint to his elder namesake that he would never be saluted as Pippin, King of the Franks.

This exclusion doubtless galled the firstborn; and to these wrongs of his, real or imaginary, appear to have been added some inflicted on him and on his friends and followers by the unloved Fastrada. Thus, while most of the other chroniclers can see in the conspiracy of Pippin only the unholy attempt of a bastard, like another Abimelech, to seize the royal power at the cost of the lives of all his legitimate brethren, the honest Einhard in the following passage of his annals puts a different colour on the enterprise.

"When the king was spending his summer at Ratisbon, a conspiracy was made against him by his eldest son, named Pippin, and certain Franks who declared that they could not bear the cruelty of the queen Fastrada, and therefore conspired for the death of the king. And when this was detected by means of Fardulf the Lombard, he, to reward him for his loyalty, was presented with the monastery of St. Dionysius [St. Denis], but the authors of the conspiracy, as being guilty of treason, were partly slain by the sword and partly hung from gallows, and so with their lives paid forfeit for the meditation of such a crime."

Pippin's own life was spared, but his head was shorn, and he was sent "to serve God in a monastery." The place of his confinement was Prum in the Moselle country, and there apparently he remained till his death, which happened in 811. So ended the last and probably the most dangerous of the conspiracies against King Charles's life and government.

CHAPTER VIII

THOUGH the greater part of his life was passed in war, and though he was undoubtedly a man of great personal courage, Charlemagne cannot be considered a great military commander. We have the testimony of Einhard that in the whole long Saxon war he himself was personally engaged in only two pitched battles, and most of his campaigns seem to have consisted rather of military promenades, against brave but ill-armed foes, than of hard-fought battles in which the genius and courage of the king at a critical moment secured victory to his troops. But if not a great captain, he was a great and successful planner of campaigns; not so much a Hannibal or a Napoleon as an "organiser of victory" like Carnot.

It is remarkable that in the most famous battle which he fought, neither his strategy nor his tactics were successful. The Spanish campaign of 778 was a failure, and ended with an event of no great importance in itself, but of imperishable memory in song, the disastrous day of Roncesvalles.

To understand the cause of this expedition, so remote

from the usual orbit of the Frankish king, we must glance for a moment at the condition of the Mohammedan world, and must leave the marshes and forests of Saxonland for the desert-girdled gardens of the oldest of cities, Damascus. For a hundred years the Ommayad caliphs in a long line, consisting of Moawiyah and thirteen successors, had governed the vast regions which owned the faith of Mohammed, with absolute sway. The caliph, as the successor of the Prophet, wielded a power religious as well as military; he was at once the pope and the emperor of the Saracen world. It was in the name of the Ommayad caliph and by his lieutenants that Spain was conquered; in his name that Gaul was invaded by those swarming myriads whom Charles Martel with difficulty repulsed on the great day of Poitiers. But now at last in the year 750, eighteen years before the accession of Charlemagne, there had come a change; the unity of Islamism was broken and the divisions that thus crept in, even more than the sword of Charles Martel, saved Europe from Moslem domination. The Ommayad caliphs in the luxurious delights of Damascus had forgotten some of the stern simplicity of their earlier predecessors. A new and more austere claimant to their religious throne presented himself in the person of Abul Abbas, who was descended from an uncle of the Prophet; and the old feud between the two tribes of the Koreish and the Haschimites flared up into fierce civil war, the reigning Ommayads belonging to the former, and the revolting Abbasides to the latter class. In the great battle of Mosul (750), the Abbasides gained the upper hand; Merwan the last Ommayad caliph fled to Egypt, where he was slain, and a bloody

massacre of eighty Ommayads at a banquet completed
the ruin of the family.

From this ruin of a princely race one only escaped.
The young Abderrahman son of Merwan fled from
Syria, and after many adventures and many narrow
escapes, ever journeying westward, reached the tents
of a tribe of Bedouins in Morocco with whom he claimed
kinship through his mother, and who gladly granted
him the asylum which he needed. While he was
sharing their hospitality, there came an embassy from
some of the chief Mussulmans of Spain to offer him
supreme power in that country. The various *emirs* and
walis who had been misgoverning that unhappy land
for forty years since the Moorish conquest, had given
it neither prosperity nor peace; probably also there
was a feeling that they had failed as champions of
Islamism against Christianity. At any rate there was
a strong desire to try what unity and concentration
under a resident and independent sovereign would
accomplish, and for this purpose to take advantage of
the presence of a high-spirited and courageous youth,
the descendant of a long line of sovereigns. The
invitation was gladly accepted. Abderrahman crossed
over into Spain (755), won victory after victory over
the representatives of his Abbaside foe, the chief of
whom was named Yussuf-el-Fekri, and (though he did
not himself assume the title of caliph), virtually founded
the Caliphate of Cordova which, for nearly three centuries, often with brilliant success, guided the destinies
of Mohammedan Spain.

But Abderrahman, though deservedly one of the
favourite heroes of Saracen literature, did not win

supreme power in Spain without a hard struggle, and
even after he had conquered there was many a fresh
outbreak of opposition to his rule. Though Yussuf-el-
Fekri fell in battle (759), his sons, continually rebelling
and continually pardoned by the magnanimous Abderrahman, filled the next twenty years with turmoil.
It was one of these sons and a son-in-law of Yussuf
who, together with a certain Ibn-el-Arabi (perhaps
the governor of Barcelona), sought out Charles while
he was holding his *placitum* at distant Paderborn, and
begged his assistance against Abderrahman, promising
that they would procure the surrender of several cities
in Spain if he appeared in arms at their gates.

The offer came during one of those deceptive lulls in
the Saxon war, when Charles was flattered with the
hope that his work was completed. It was from this
very assembly that Widukind was conspicuously absent,
but Charles knew not as yet how much that absence
imported. The offer was a tempting one and harmonised
with Charles's general policy. Abderrahman was the
enemy of the Abbaside caliph, and the Abbasides were
Charles's friends. There was, too, a prospect of continuing the work which his father had so prosperously
begun when he won back Narbonne from the infidels.
As he listened, the three Mussulmans enlarged on the
brilliant prospect before him, and very probably held
out hopes of the conquest of the whole peninsula. The
question of the rival faiths, though of course it must
have been present to Charles's mind, does not seem to
have been the determining motive to this expedition as
it was to the Saxon war. There is no foundation for
the suggestion of some later chroniclers that he was

moved to this enterprise by pity for the groans of the
Spanish Christians under Saracen oppression. In fact,
the situation of the Christians under Abderrahman
seems to have been a very tolerable one : and as we
shall see, the valiant little kingdom of the Asturias,
which from its mountain stronghold was so gallantly
maintaining the cause of Christian freedom against the
Moors, got small help at this time from its mighty co-
religionist.

Whatever the cause, Charles determined to accept
the invitation to interfere in the affairs of the Spanish
peninsula. At Easter (778) he was at Chasseneuil, in
Aquitaine, about forty miles south of his grandfather's
battle-field at Poitiers. He opened his campaign early :
of course the warmer climate of Spain justified much
earlier operations than were possible in the late spring
of undrained Saxon-land. Having spent the winter in
preparations he had a large army at his disposal, and
dividing it according to his usual custom, he ordered the
Austrasian part of it to cross the Eastern Pyrenees. In
this division of the army there were not only, as we might
naturally expect, men of Septimania, of Provence and
Burgundy, but some of Charles's new Lombard subjects
from Italy : and even a contingent sent by the Bavarian
Tassilo. Charles himself, with the western portion of
his army, marched probably by the old Roman road,
passing from St. Jean de la Port over a crest of the
Pyrenees 5000 feet high, into that which has since
become the kingdom of Navarre. The highest point of
this road, the "Summus Pyreneus" of the Roman road-
books, looked down on the wild and narrow defile of
Roncesvalles.

It had been ordered that the two sections of the army should meet at Cæsar-Augusta, now Saragossa, on the Ebro. Both sections appear to have crossed the Pyrenees without difficulty, and Charles, descending into Navarre, laid siege to Pampelona and took it apparently with little difficulty. The reader learns with some surprise that Pampelona had previously belonged to the little Christian kingdom of the Asturias, against whom Charles must therefore have now been waging war.

And this was really the only warlike deed in the whole campaign: for all the rest of the operations recorded by the chroniclers (who evidently have something to conceal in this part of their story) cannot be dignified by the name of war. Charles is said to have crossed the Ebro by a ford, to have approached, perhaps entered, Saragossa, to have received the hostages whom Ibn - el - Arabi and another Saracen chief whom the chronicler calls Abuthaur (probably Abu Taker) brought to him. No doubt the hostages represented the surrender of a certain number of cities in the corner of Spain between the Ebro and the Pyrenees, but how many we have no means of deciding. In the month of August Charles set out on his return march, taking Ibn-el-Arabi with him in chains. Evidently the expedition had been a comparative failure: the large promises of Ibn-el-Arabi had not been fulfilled, and Charles, resentful, perhaps suspecting treachery, determined not to suffer the evil counsellor to be at large.

The cause of the failure was probably in part to be found in the premature rising of Abderrahman-ibn-Habib, son-in-law of Yussuf, who, before Charles entered Spain, had landed in Murcia with an army of Berbers,

and had raised the standard of the Abbaside caliphs
against his namesake Abderrahman-ben-Merwan. The
utter failure of this expedition probably made it hopeless
for Charles to proceed beyond the Ebro.

Returning to Pampelona Charles levelled the walls
of that city to the ground, to prevent its rebelling
against him, and then began his march across the
Pyrenees. On the highest point of the pass an ambush
had been planted by the Wascones whose operations
were concealed by the dense forests growing there.
When the baggage-train and rear-guard came in sight
they dashed down upon them. The surprise and the
possession of the higher ground fully compensated for
the mountaineers' inferiority in arms and discipline; in
fact, in such an encounter the heavier armour of the
Franks was a positive disadvantage. By the confession
of the biographer of Charlemagne at least the whole of
the rear-guard were cut to pieces, and with them fell
many of the nobles of Charles's court, notably Eggihard
the seneschal, Anselm the count of the palace, and
Hruodland the governor of the Breton March. As
night soon fell and the nimble invaders dispersed rapidly
to their homes and hiding-places, revenge was impossible,
and Charles returned to Chasseneuil with clouded brow,
all his satisfaction at his successes in Spain—such as
they were—being marred by this dishonour to his arms
and by the loss of so many of his friends.

The date of this disaster is fixed by the epitaph of
the seneschal Eggihard to the 18th of August 778.
The place, by undeviating tradition, has been identified
with the wild gorge of Roncesvalles. It is indeed
somewhat difficult to understand how even the main

body of the Frankish army could have escaped, if the
foes were on the very summit of the pass, and if the
skirmish took place at Roncesvalles on the Spanish side
of the mountain : but this may be accounted for by the
distance at which the baggage-train and the rear-guard
lagged behind the van.

It was at this same point of the Pyrenean ridge and
through this same defile of Roncesvalles that Soult's
gallant soldiers forced their way in 1813, when the
French marshal made his brilliant, but unsuccessful,
attempt to turn Wellington's position and raise the siege
of Pampelona.

But who were these Wascones, and what was their
quarrel with Charles ? Certainly they were not Saracens
or Mussulmans as the minstrels of later centuries supposed.   A part of the mysterious Basque race, which has
throughout the historic period occupied the high upland
valleys on either side of the Western Pyrenees, and has
given its name to Biscay in Spain and to Gascony in
France, these mountaineers represent probably the oldest
population of Europe of which any traces now remain.
Their language, bearing no relation to any Aryan or
Semitic tongue, is to this day one of the great unsolved
enigmas of philology.   As has been said, they were
certainly not Mussulmans, and they may have professed
and called themselves Christians, but it is not necessary
to seek for any deep political combination, Christian or
Mohammedan, to account for their attack on Charles's
baggage-train.   The men whose ancestors had been
driven, perhaps two thousand years before, into those
mountains by the Celts, were determined, and had been
determined ever since, to keep their last asylum free

from the foot of the invader. Roman and Goth had
vainly tried to subdue them, and now this Frankish
interloper should have a lesson that should prevent his
paying too frequent visits to their mountains. Theirs
was a savage love, not merely of independence but of
absolute isolation: that, and the attractions of the
Frankish baggage-train seem quite sufficient to account
for the disaster of Roncesvalles.

Among the nobles who fell was, as has been said,
Hruodland, governor of the Breton March. This is
none other than the far-famed Roland of mediæval
romance. The minstrels and *trouveurs* of much later
centuries have invented for him a relationship to Charlemagne, have mated him with Oliver, and have said a
thousand beautiful things concerning his life and his
heroic death; but, of all this, authentic history knows
nothing. And yet authentic history cannot afford
altogether to ignore even the Roland of romance, since
it was—

> De L'Allemaigne et de Rollant
> Et d'Olivier et de Vassaux
> Qui morurent en Rainschevaux,

that Norman Taillefer sang as he spurred his horse and
tossed his sword aloft before the battle of Hastings.
Even the mythical Roland had become, three centuries
after the rout of Roncesvalles, a great name to conjure
with.

As for Charles's attempt to annex territory to his
kingdom south of the Pyrenees, it had to be abandoned
for a time. The Saxon revolt under Widukind broke
out, more stubborn and difficult to quell than ever. For
the next eight years (778-785) Charles was too much

occupied with the hard reality of strife in the marshes and forests of Saxon-land to have leisure for pursuing a visionary sovereignty on the banks of the Ebro. Then came the trouble with Tassilo, and, immediately following upon it, those wars with the Avars which will be described in the next chapter. But though during this period most or all of the cities in Spain which had accepted Charles as their lord were probably won back by Abderrahman, the hope of reconquering a Spanish kingdom was never abandoned, and the execution of the scheme was committed to the King of Aquitaine, or rather to his counsellors. For this King of Aquitaine was Charles's fourth son Louis, who with a twin brother had been born in 778, while Charles himself was prosecuting the war in Spain. Born in Aquitaine, this child —one day to be the gentle and much worried Emperor, Louis the Pious—was, as we have seen, when only three years old, anointed in Rome by the pope as king of his native land : and in that land his boyhood and early manhood appear to have been spent. During those years of immaturity the government was of course in the hands of counsellors, who seem to have executed the commands of the real ruler Charles with vigour and prudence.

In 788 Abderrahman died, and was succeeded by his youngest son Hescham, a Mussulman pietist. The fierce, and for the time successful, invasion of the Narbonese province which was made by Hescham's general Abd-el-Melec, was perhaps the cause which stirred Louis's council to commence a war of reprisals. In 796 the country of the Saracens was ravaged by a Frankish army. In 797 Huesca was besieged, but in vain. In 801 Barcelona, which had changed hands two or three times between Christian and Mussulman, was subjected to a rigorous siege, which lasted according to one account seven months, and according to another two years. The city was at last forced to surrender, and Zaid, its governor, who had in former years played fast and loose with the Frankish alliance, was sent in chains to Charles's court. Between 809 and 811 there were three attempts, the last a successful attempt, to capture Tortosa, the strong city which commanded the mouth of the Ebro. All these conquests seem to have been retained during the lifetime of Charles. What was perhaps more important, a firm alliance was formed with the young Alfonso the Chaste, who, during his fifty years' reign (791-842) extended the frontiers and consolidated the strength of the Christian kingdom of the Asturias. This alliance, so obviously for the interest of both parties, cannot have existed in the year of Roncesvalles : but now we are told that " there came to the court of Charles an ambassador of Hadefonsus, King of Gallicia and the Asturias, presenting a tent of wonderful beauty," and that " Charles so bound Hadefonsus to him as an ally that the latter whenever he sent him letters or ambassadors would never allow himself to be called anything else than ' King Charles's own man.' "

At first sight the result of these wars beyond the Pyrenees, and the consequent foundation of the Spanish March, which stretched from those mountains to the Ebro, may seem unimportant, as we know that the Frankish kings made no permanent acquisition of territory in Spain. But on the other hand, by the diversion which they caused, they perhaps prevented the

Saracen rulers of Spain from crushing the infant kingdom of the Asturias : and the counts of Barcelona, whom they settled in the Spanish March, after having gradually relinquished the position of vassals to the French kings, became independent Christian sovereigns, and eventually acquired by marriage the rich heritage of the kingdom of Aragon.

CHAPTER IX

WARS WITH AVARS AND SCLAVES

IT is a remarkable ethnological fact, and one for which there does not seem any obvious explanation, that, almost ever since the great barbarian migrations of the fourth century, the country between the Danube and the Carpathian mountains has been occupied by a people belonging to that which, for want of a better word, we call the Turanian stock; and yet that this Turanian deposit should not have been one and the same throughout, but was the result of three distinct migrations. In the fourth century the great non-Aryan nation on the Middle Danube was the Huns; from the tenth century to the present day it has been that noble nation whom their Sclavonic neighbours have named Hungarians, but who call themselves Magyars; between 567 and 800, it was the savage and somewhat uninteresting people of the Avars. The power of the Avars was at its height in the reign of the emperor Heraclius (626) when they formed the siege of Constantinople, and, joining hands with the Persians, had well-nigh accomplished the ruin of the eastern Empire. Soon after this came the revolt of the Bulgarians from the Avar sway, and from that time onward, the power of the Avars steadily declined, but though no longer formidable to Constantinople they were still securely quartered in the vast plains of Hungary, and were most unwelcome neighbours to their old allies the Lombards of Italy. Twice in the course ·of the seventh century had they descended upon the duchy of Friuli, and each time their invasions had been marked by that character of destruction and purposeless brutality which has ever been the especial note of the Tartar conqueror.

If the Avars were at all like their Hunnish kinsmen (which is not improbable) they were small of stature, and swarthy in colour. Their long locks hanging down behind, in a kind of woven pigtails, are specially noticed by the Frankish poets. They were essentially a predatory nation, and (again arguing from the analogy of the Huns) we may presume that they were a nation of horsemen, dashing hither and thither on their nimble and hardy ponies, and vanishing ere the heavy squadrons of the Greeks or the Lombards could come up with them. They had one chief ruler, who was called the *chagan* of the Avars—the same title with which we are familiar as the Tartar khan—and under him, in a degree of subordination which it would be hopeless now to determine, were lieutenants or sub-kings, who bore the title of *tudun.* We hear also of the *jugur,* apparently not a proper name, but the title of a chief who contests the supremacy with the *chagan. Tarchan* seems to be a collective word for the Avar nobility.

The capital of the Avars consisted of a series of earthworks, which were known (probably to their German neighbours, not to themselves) by the collective name of the *Hring*. Of this Hring an interesting description is given by the monk of St. Gall, who wrote some ninety years after its destruction, but who professes to tell the story as he heard it in his boyhood from an old soldier named Adalbert, who had served in the Avar campaigns. With a charming touch of nature, the old monk describes how the veteran used to prose on about his warlike experiences, and how he as a boy resisted, and often escaped from the tedious tale, but yet was in the end forced to listen and to learn.

He says: "The land of the Huns [or Avars] as Adalbert used to tell me was girdled with nine circles. Then said I, who had never seen any circles [circular fences] except those made of osiers, 'What sort of marvel was that, sir?' and he answered, 'It was fortified with nine *hegin*.' I, who had never seen any hedges except those with which the crops are guarded, asked him some more questions, and he said, 'One circle was as wide as the distance from Zurich to Constance [thirty miles]: it was made of stems of oak, beech, or fir, twenty feet high, and twenty feet broad. All the hollow part [between the walls] was filled either with very hard stones, or with most tenacious chalk, and then the top of the structure was covered with strong turfs. In between the turfs were planted shrubs which were pruned and lopped, so as to make them shoot forth boughs and leaves. Between one mound and another the villages and farms were placed, always within earshot of one another; and opposite to them, the walls (in themselves impregnable) were pierced by narrow gateways, through which the inhabitants, both those who lived in the inner circle and those who were in the outer ring, used to sally forth for the sake of plunder. From the second circle, which was constructed like the first, there was a distance of twenty Teutonic or forty Italian miles to the third, and so on to the ninth, though [of course], each successive circle was smaller than the one before it. And from circle to circle the farms and dwellings were so arranged on all sides, that an alarm could be given by sound of the trumpet from each circle to its neighbour."

It is easy to see that this description cannot be scientifically accurate (the distance between the "rings" especially must be greatly over-stated): but still, this sketch of the camp-city of a robber horde, entrenched in the plains of Hungary in order to make war on the growing civilisation of the west, is surely worthy of our attention, and helps us to understand what were the difficulties of Charles and his subject princes in breaking the power of this barbarous race.

It will be remembered that one of the grounds of accusation against the insubordinate Duke of Bavaria was, that he had been intriguing with the Avars against his lord. It is probable that, sooner or later, when he found Charles bent on his destruction, Tassilo did make overtures of some kind for a league of mutual defence with his formidable eastern neighbours. Certain it is that they came, though too late to help him, with two armies against the Franks (788). One army went southward against the duchy of Friuli, the other westward against Bavaria. Both were defeated, the latter at Ips on the Danube (about forty miles south of Linz), having only just touched the frontier of Bavaria. Enraged at meeting such a hostile reception from the Bavarians

whom, as they said, they came to help, they made
another invasion later in the same year; but the two
brave *missi* of Charles, Grahamann and Audacer, who
had repelled the previous invasion now again won a
signal victory. Great was the slaughter on the field,
and multitudes of the flying Avars were whelmed in
the waters of the Danube.

It is probable that Charles was already revolving in
his mind plans for the entire subjugation of the
barbarous Avar nationality, but he knew that such an
enterprise would require long preparations, and meanwhile events were again occurring on the Elbe which
required his immediate attention. The Saxons, it is
true, were still apparently submissive to the yoke—we
are now in that seven years' peace (785-792) which
followed the submission of Widukind—but there was a
fierce and warlike Sclavonic tribe called by themselves
Welatabi, but by the Franks Wiltzi, who dwelt beyond
the Elbe in the country which has since been named
Pomerania, and these people, having by the subjugation
of the Saxons become next-door neighbours to the
Frankish State, were displaying those qualities which
generally bring the less civilised race into collision with
the more civilised, when a narrow boundary divides
them. As the chronicler puts it : "This people was ever
hostile to the Franks, and was wont to pursue with
their hatred, to oppress and harass in war all their
neighbours who were either subject to the Franks or in
league with them. Whose insolence the king thought
he ought no longer to put up with, and he therefore
determined to attack them in war, and, having collected
a large army, he crossed the Danube at Cologne" (789).

He marched through Saxon-land, crossed the Elbe by two bridges, led his army (in whose ranks fought many of the lately subdued Saxons), into the hostile territory, and, according to the usual formula, laid everything waste with fire and sword. The Wiltzi, though a warlike people, lost heart, and when the oldest and most powerful of their chiefs, a man named Dragawit, came in and made his submission to Charles, all the others followed his example. There were the usual oaths of vassalage, surrender of hostages, perhaps a promise of tribute : but although, from the way in which it is mentioned by Charles's biographer it is evident that this campaign against the Wiltzi was an arduous one, it cannot be said to have produced any enduring results. Speaking generally, the Elbe remained the boundary of the Frankish kingdom. The various Sclavonic tribes on the other side of it were, to borrow a term from modern diplomacy, " in the Frankish sphere of influence," but they were not obedient citizens of the Frankish state.

We return to the affairs of the Avars. The year 790 was a quiet one, so much so that Charles, now verging on his fiftieth year, and "fearing to grow torpid through lack of exercise," sailed up the Main and the Franconian Saale to his palace of Königshofen by the banks of the latter river, and returned in like manner to Worms. But even in this year there were discussions and altercations concerning boundaries with the ambassadors of the Avars. Charles was evidently making his preparations and accumulating materials for his case against the doomed nationality.

Next year, 791, the storm burst, and Charles made

his great, his only personally commanded expedition, into Avar-land. At a council of Franks, Saxons, and Frisians held at Ratisbon, it was decided that "on account of the great and intolerable malice which the Avars had shown towards the Holy Church and the Christian people, and the impossibility of obtaining justice at their hands by means of the royal messengers, a hostile expedition should march against them." The whole army marched to the river Enns, the boundary of Avar-land, and there for three days sang litanies and witnessed solemn masses imploring God "for the safety of the army, the help of our Lord Jesus Christ, and victory and vengeance against the Avars." Charles then, according to his usual custom, divided his army, marching himself along the south bank of the Danube, and sending the Saxon and Frisian auxiliaries with some Franks along the northern bank. The Avars had erected two strongholds, one on each side of the river, at a little distance above the modern city of Vienna: but they were struck with panic fear when they saw the two columns marching on either side of the river, and the ships (laden probably with provisions) sailing majestically between them. They abandoned their strongholds without striking a blow, "and so, Christ leading on his own people, both armies entered the country without sustaining any loss." It was, in fact, a military promenade. Charles marched through the country, ravaging as he went, as far as the river Raab, and then, "after traversing and laying waste a great part of Pannonia, carried back his army safe and sound into Bavaria. This expedition was made without inconvenience of any kind, save that in that part of the army which the king commanded, so great a pestilence arose among the horses that scarcely the tenth part out of so many thousands of horses is said to have remained alive." The king returned to Ratisbon, which he evidently intended now to make his headquarters till the end of the Avar war, and kept his Christmas there.

Next year, however (792), broke out the conspiracy of Pippin the Hunchback, and this probably occupied so much of Charles's attention as to make it impossible to undertake an expedition into Avar-land. He remained, however, during the whole year in Bavaria, and ordered the construction of a bridge of boats which he might in the next campaign throw across the Danube, and so at any moment unite the two armies marching along the opposite banks of the river.

In 793 came the terrible tidings of the destruction of Theodoric's army by the banks of the Weser, and the rekindling of the Saxon war, deadlier and fiercer than ever. The abortive attempt to canalise the feeders of the Danube and the Rhine, and so unite those two great arteries of his kingdom, occupied Charles all the summer of that year. On its failure he recognised that the war against the Avars must be suspended for a season, at any rate as far as his personal share in it was concerned. He set his face northward and made Frankfurt, Aachen, and the towns of Saxon-land itself, his abiding places during the six years that followed.

But it seems that the great campaign of 791 had been even more successful than it was thought to be at the time. There appear to have been jealousies and rivalries in the Avar kingdom which, as soon as the restraint of fear was removed, as soon as it was seen

that the *chagan* was not invincible, broke forth into
open dissension and completed the wreck of the
barbarous state. In the summer of 795, while Charles,
keenly intent on the Saxon war, was encamped by the
Elbe in a place near to the present site of Lüneburg,
there came to him messengers from a *tudun* of the
Avars announcing his willingness to be baptized and to
hand over his people and land to the Frankish king.
And in fact next year this *tudun* came according to
his promise to Aachen, and there made his formal
submission to Charles. He and his followers were
baptized and returned home enriched by royal gifts.

But meanwhile there had been more evident tokens
of the utter collapse of the Avar kingdom. The conduct
of the war after Charles's departure had apparently
been left to the Duke of Friuli, who inherited the
hatred of two centuries of border wars between his
duchy and the Avars. The duke now ruling was a
Frank named Eric, a man distinguished in the wars,
and who might truly be called a Paladin of Charles's
court, but also a generous benefactor of the poor, a
friend of the Church, a man to whom Paulinus, Bishop
of Aquileia, addressed a treatise on practical religion
(perhaps something like Jeremy Taylor's treatise on
Holy Living), evidently with the assurance that it would
meet with a hearty welcome from his friend. This
devout and valiant warrior, in the late autumn of 795,
invaded Avar-land, penetrated to the far-famed *Hring*,
pierced through all its seven circles, and made himself
master of the immense hoard which the *chagans* had been
piling up there for two centuries. It was no wonder
that he found an enormous accumulation of treasure,

for, besides the results of the mere robber raids which the predatory Avars had made on all the surrounding peoples, during a great part of the seventh century the eastern emperors had been forced to pay 80,000 or 100,000 golden *solidi* as a yearly tribute to these terrible neighbours; nay, on one occasion the Emperor Heraclius had to purchase peace from them at the price of 200,000 *solidi*. The locking up of such a vast quantity of the only considerable European currency in this barbarian stronghold must have sensibly affected the economic condition of Europe, and it would not be surprising if future inquirers should discover that there was a great rise of prices as the consequence of its dispersion. Besides the hoarded *solidi* there were gorgeous arms, silken tissues, and many other precious things; and all these, according to one annalist, were sent piled on fifteen great waggons, each drawn by four oxen, to Charles at Aachen. The courtiers and nobles received generous presents from the king out of the great hoard; the pope and his chief ecclesiastical friends were not forgotten, but much also was laid up in the royal treasury and not distributed till the king's death.

In the next year (796) Charles's son Pippin, King of Italy, followed up Eric's success; again visited the mysterious *Hring* to complete the work of spoliation, drove the Avars across the Theiss, and visited his father at Aachen, bringing with him the plunder of the conquered people.

There were indeed some upflickerings of the apparently extinguished fire. The baptized *tudun* failed to keep his oath of fealty to Charles, and had to be punished for his perfidy. In 799 Gerold, the Frankish governor of Bavaria, brother of Charles's late queen Hildegard, fell in battle with the insurgent Avars. But this Turanian people made not near so obstinate or long continued a resistance as the Teutonic Saxons. In the year 805 we find the *capchan*, who was a Christian, and bore the Greek name Theodore, humbly petitioning the Emperor Charles that on account of the needs of his people a place of habitation might be assigned to them between Sabaria and Carnuntum (the country round the Neusiedler See). His request was granted, and he returned to his people enriched by presents from the emperor, but soon after died. The new *chagan* soon after "sent one of his nobles praying that he might have the ancient honour which the *chagan* used to have among the Avars. To which prayer the emperor gave his assent, and ordered that the *chagan* should have the supremacy over the whole kingdom according to the old custom of the Avars."

After this we practically hear no more of the Avars during the lifetime of Charles. The power of the great Turanian kingdom was utterly broken, and possibly, but for the invasion of the Hungarians, who appeared upon the scene about seventy years after the death of Charlemagne, there would have been a complete reconquest of the lands of the Middle Danube by the Teutonic race. It must not be forgotten, however, that here, as well as further north, Sclavonic tribes were hovering round the eastern border of the Frankish kingdom, and, in fact, it was in a war with one of these tribes, the Croatian inhabitants of Tarsatica, on the Adriatic, that the valiant Eric of Friuli lost his life (799). The news was brought to King Charles at Paderborn at the same time as the tidings of the death of his brother-in-law, Gerold, and saddened him in the midst of his Saxon victories. Bishop Paulinus wrote a Latin elegy on the death of his friend, in which, like David in his lament over Saul, he prayed that neither dew nor rain might fall on the Liburnian shore, nor corn nor wine might gladden the hills on which the noble Eric met his doom.

CHAPTER X

Now that we are approaching the most important event in the life of Charlemagne, his assumption of the imperial title, it will be necessary to glance at his relations with the line of sovereigns who alone up to the year 800 wore the title of Emperor, the Cæsars of Constantinople.

It will be hardly needful here to repeat the warning given by many recent historians against considering the State which was governed from Constantinople, between 476 and 800, as anything else than the *Roman* empire. As its centre of gravity was now on the Bosphorus instead of being on the Tiber, and as its chief possessions were situated on the east of the Gulf of Venice, or even on the east of the Archipelago, it is difficult to avoid speaking of it as the eastern empire ; but for all the centuries between the fifth and the ninth we must remember that this is not a strictly accurate expression. It was during all that period "*the empire*," "the dominion of the world," nay, it was still the "Roman republic," though the man who sat in Julius Cæsar's seat was practically the uncontrolled despot of the Roman world.

And during all these intermediate centuries, though the empire might be cut very short, by Frank and Goth and Saxon in the west, or by the Saracen in the east, it would be safe to say that it never acquiesced in its limitations. Pre-eminently the wonderful reconquests of Italy, of Africa, of part of Spain, which were wrought in the sixth century by the generals of Justinian, might well keep alive the hope that, after the "little systems" of barbarian and infidel had "had their day," the true Divinely-appointed world-ruler would emerge from his temporary eclipse and be again supreme all round the shores of the Mediterranean.

Doubtless, though the name "Roman" was still kept and still gloried in, the empire was, with each succeeding century, becoming more thoroughly Greek, or rather Graeco-Asiatic, in its character. From this point of view it has been observed by a modern historian that the great pestilence which raged in 747 (five years after the birth of Charles) was an important factor in the transformation of the empire. "A vast portion of the inhabitants of Byzantium, who maintained Roman character and many Roman traditions amid all their half-Hellenic, half-Oriental ways, had been carried off by the plague, and were replaced by pure Greeks who had not inherited the effect of Roman influence. This was an important step in the direction of becoming a Greek nationality, to which goal the Roman empire was steadily tending" (Bury, *History of the Later Roman Empire*, ii. 456).

But, notwithstanding this, the emperor at Byzantium never forgot that he was Roman, but always looked upon Italy as his lawful, his almost inalienable, possession. Gaul, Spain, Britain—it might be necessary to abandon these to the barbarians—but Italy, but Rome, were rightfully his, and all the shades of all the buried Cæsars would pass in angry procession before the eyes of the degenerate successor who should be so base as formally to abandon his right to hold them. This, or something like this, we may believe to have been the secret underlying thought of the Leos and the Constantines when they heard what the Frank was doing in Italy.

Through the greater part of the eighth century the Iconoclastic controversy was the dominating element in the politics of the empire. We have already seen something of the career of the first great image-breaker, Leo III. On his death, which happened in 740 (two years before the birth of Charlemagne) he was succeeded by his son Constantine V., as able a general, as strong a statesman, and as determined an image-breaker as his father. He was a great enemy also of the monks, and both they and the image-worshippers suffered at his hands a persecution which (at any rate according to their account of it) might seem to recall the days of Decius and Diocletian.

To the court of Constantine V. fled the young Adelchis, son of Desiderius, on the downfall of the Lombard kingdom (774). He was well received by the emperor, who bestowed upon him the high-sounding title of Patrician, thus making him, as far as rank in the empire went, at least the equal of his conqueror, Charles. We have seen how the combination of rebellious Italian dukes, independent princes, and Byzantine generals, which was formed to restore Adelchis to the Lombard throne, failed, owing to the death of Constantine V. (September 775), and how Hrodgaud of Friuli was left alone to bear and to sink under the vengeful might of the Frankish king.

The Emperor Constantine V. was succeeded by his son Leo IV., surnamed the Khazar, his mother having been a princess of that barbarous Tartar tribe, who dwelt by the Sea of Azof and under the Caucasus. The strain of barbarian blood did not bring strength to the character of the young emperor. Leo IV., though an earnest image-breaker, was distinctly a weaker man than his father, and during his short reign the cause of Iconoclasm probably retrograded rather than advanced.

The five years during which Leo the Khazar was on the throne (775-780) were years during which Charles gave little attention to the affairs of Italy, having much to occupy him elsewhere, for these were the years of Roncesvalles and of the fresh outbreak of the Saxon revolt. His friend and clamorous dependant, however, Pope Hadrian, sent him frequent cries for help. "The Greeks hateful to God" (that is the generals and ministers of Leo the Khazar) were conspiring with the "most unutterable" Lombards of Benevento to seduce the towns in Campania from their allegiance to Charles and Hadrian. The island of Sicily, the one secure stronghold of the Byzantine power during all these centuries, was the focus of this strife, but in order to prosecute it more successfully the patrician of Sicily took up his headquarters at Gaeta, and from thence, in concert with the Duke of Naples, was pressing hard upon those Campanian and Latian cities which kept their loyalty to the pope. Moreover, when Hadrian wrote one of his most urgent letters, in 779, it was daily expected that "the son of the most unutterable and long ago absolutely unmentionable king Desiderius" would land in Italy with soldiers lent him by his Imperial ally and head the anti-Papal, anti-Frankish coalition.

Still, however, Adelchis lingered in Constantinople and once again a vacancy in the palace of the Cæsars saved Italy from a war. On the 8th of September 780, Leo the Khazar died and was succeeded by his son Constantine VI., a boy of nine years old, ruling not under the regency of, but jointly with, his mother Irene. This woman was a daughter of Athens and a secret worshipper of images, though in her father-in-law's lifetime she had solemnly sworn always to adhere to the party of. the Iconoclasts. Like Queen Athaliah of old, she was passionately fond of power, both for its own sake and as helping her to maintain the cause of idolatry against the religious reformers, and she was ready, in defence of her darling schemes of ambition, to violate not only the oath which she had given to her father-in-law—that was a light and pardonable offence—but the deepest and holiest instincts of a woman's heart, the love of a mother for her only son.

For the first ten years of the joint reign (780-790) the lad, Constantine VI., quietly submitted to his mother's ascendency, and only her will and her projects require the historian's attention. The Iconoclastic spirit was strong among the soldiers of her late husband's family, and she had to wait four years before she could openly take steps towards the restoration of the worship of images; but she seems at once to have ceased the attacks on Hadrian's subject cities, and to have assumed a more friendly attitude towards Charles, who was not

himself at this time interested in the Iconoclastic controversy, but whose friendship was important if the
Patriarchate of Constantinople was to be reconciled with
that of Rome.   Thus it came to pass that in 781, during
Charles's second visit to Rome, there appeared in that
city two high nobles of the Byzantine Court, the *sacellarius* Constans and the *primicerius* Mamalus, who brought
proposals for a marriage between the young emperor
and Charles's daughter Hrotrud, whom the Greeks called
Eruthro.   It was only an alliance at some future day
that was talked of, for the prospective bridegroom was
but ten years old, and the Frankish princess was probably about eight.   But the match was a splendid one,
there having been no previous instance of a matrimonial
alliance between the Roman Cæsars and the Frankish
kings, and Charles gladly accepted the offer.   A tutor
named Elissæus was sent to the Frankish court to
instruct the future empress in the Greek tongue, and
there was peace in Italy between the Franks and the
generals of the empire.

During these years of peace Irene was maturing her
plans for the restoration of image-worship.   In 784,
Paul the Patriarch of Constantinople resigned his great
office and became a monk, acknowledging to all the
world that his conscience was troubled by the isolation
of Constantinople from all the other Patriarchates on
the ground of Iconoclasm.   Nothing could have suited
Irene's plans better than this resignation.   Her secretary
Tarasius, though a layman, was made patriarch in the
room of Paul, evidently on the understanding that
images were to be restored.   In August 785 an imperial
letter from Constantine and Irene was addressed to

Pope Hadrian begging him to fix a time for the convoca-
tion of a general council at Constantinople to settle the
question of Iconoclasm. The pope of course gladly consented, though he took advantage of the reopened
intercourse with Constantinople to demand the restoration of the "patrimonies" (probably in Sicily) which
had been taken away from St. Peter's see by the first
Iconoclastic emperor: and though he also held up to
the Byzantine rulers the admirable example of Charles,
"King of the Franks and Lombards, and Patrician of
Rome, who had in all things obeyed the admonitions of
the pope his spiritual father, had subdued to himself
the barbarous nations of the west, and had given back
to the church of St. Peter many estates, provinces, and
towns, of which it had been despoiled by the faithless
Lombards."

The general council was opened at Constantinople in
August 786, but failed of its purpose. The Iconoclastic
spirit was still too strong among the soldiers who were
quartered in Constantinople, old comrades of Leo III.
and his son. The church was invaded by them, and
the image-worshipping bishops departed in fear. Next
year, however, care having been taken to dispose of the
Iconoclastic troops elsewhere, a general council was held
at Nicæa (24th September to 23rd October 787), and
there the *cultus* of images was re-established in full glory,
only with one of those distinctions dear to theologians
which defined "that it was right to salute and grovel in
adoration before the holy images, but not to give them
that peculiar worship which is due to God alone."

Thus, then, the great cause of ecclesiastical contention
was removed, and we might expect that the joyful event

would be celebrated by the marriage of the young
affianced pair, Constantine and Hrotrud, now aged sixteen and fourteen respectively. On the contrary, this
was the very year in which, after mysterious embassies
backwards and forwards between the two Courts, the
marriage treaty was broken off and the relations became
more openly hostile than ever; but curiously enough
(as is not unfrequently the case in such affairs) there is
a conflict of testimony as to which side had the credit
or discredit of breaking off the match. The Frankish
annalists say or hint that Charles refused his daughter
to the young Emperor, who was much angered by the
refusal. A Byzantine historian says that "Irene broke
off the treaty with the Franks and sent the Captain of
the Guard to fetch a damsel from Armenia named Mary
whom she married to her son the Emperor Constantine,
he being much grieved thereat, and not liking his bride
because his inclination was towards the daughter of
Charles, King of the Franks, to whom he had been pre-
contracted."

It is hopeless with our scanty materials to discover
the reason of this mysterious rupture between the Courts.
One of the most careful of the German writers who have
treated of this period attributes it entirely to Charles's
invasion of Benevento and reduction of its prince Arichis
to vassalage, which, as has been already related, occurred
in the year 786. This, he considers, was a breach of the
tacit agreement to maintain the Italian *status quo ante*
entered into in 781, and was resented accordingly.
Others have seen in it a stroke of policy on the part of
Irene, who was already becoming jealous of her son's
share in the Imperial authority, and feared to see him

provided with a too powerful father-in-law. If it be permitted to hazard yet another conjecture, where all is conjectural, I would point out that in the interval between 781 and 787, Hildegard, the mother of Hrotrud, had died, and Charles had married another wife, the haughty and unpopular Fastrada. Possibly that proud and jealous woman resented the idea of seeing her little step-daughter raised higher than herself by her exaltation to the throne of the Cæsars, and may have used her influence with her husband to entangle still further the already ravelled hank of the negotiations with Constantinople, and at last in disgust to break off the match altogether? The whole story is a remarkable illustration of the fact, so clearly shown in the negotiations for the Spanish marriage of Charles I. when Prince of Wales, that a marriage treaty, if not very carefully conducted, is quite as likely to embroil two sovereigns as to unite them.

One curious, though not immediate, result of the rapidly increasing estrangement between Franks and Greeks was that in the great synod which Charles held at Frankfurt in 794 for the condemnation of the " Adoptian heresy," Charles induced his bishops to pass a severe condemnation of " the synod held a few years before under Irene and her son which called itself the Seventh Ecumenical Council, but which was neither the seventh nor ecumenical, but was rejected by all present at Frankfurt as absolutely superfluous." At the same time it was declared by the assembled bishops that neither worship nor adoration was to be paid to the images of the saints. Thus was Charles, the great patron and defender of the papacy, actually brought into contro-

versy with the pope on an important point of Christian
practice.

The immediate effect of the rupture of the marriage
treaty was seen in an invasion of Italy by the Greeks,
in which at last the long lingering Adelchis took part.
The intention was to make an attack on Charles's
dominions in combination with the Prince of Benevento
(on whom the dignity of patrician was conferred) perhaps also with Tassilo the Bavarian; but before the
Imperial troops landed in Italy, Arichis of Benevento
was no more. He died on the 26th of August 787, a
man still in the flower of his age. It is striking to
observe how much Charles's upward course to empire
was facilitated by the opportune deaths of his competitors.
Carloman, Constantine V., Leo IV., and now Arichis of
Benevento, all died at the most seasonable time for the
success of Charles's projects. At the time of the death
of Arichis, his son and heir Grimwald III. was in
Charles's keeping as a hostage. Pope Hadrian earnestly
besought the king never to permit one of the God-hated
dynasty to ascend the Beneventan throne, but Charles,
after some delay, allowed Grimwald to return and take
his place in the palace of Benevento. He was, however,
compelled to promise to pay a yearly tribute of 7000
solidi, to coin money with Charles's effigy, to date his
charters by the years of the Frankish king, and in
all things to acknowledge him as his over-lord. For the
present these conditions were kept, and at the crisis of
the Byzantine invasion Grimwald III. comported himself as a loyal vassal of Charles. So it came to pass
that when at last the Byzantine troops landed in Calabria
they were met by the united forces of the Frankish

king under his general Winighis, and the Lombard
dukes of Spoleto and Benevento. The defeat of the
Greeks was crushing (788). Four thousand of their
warriors were slain, among them the *sacellarius* John,
commander of the expedition; and one thousand were
taken prisoners. Adelchis appears to have made his
escape. He reappeared no more on the soil of Italy, but
died many years after, an elderly, probably a wealthy,
patrician at Constantinople. This last scion of the
Lombard kings is not an interesting figure in history.

Charles's reply to this direct attack on his dominions
in the south of Italy was to lay hands on the Imperial
province of Istria in the north, a conquest desirable in
itself, for the cities of Istria were numerous and wealthy,
and also one that facilitated the operations which he
was planning against the Avars. The Court of Constantinople, probably dispirited by the defeat of the great
armament under the *sacellarius* John seems to have
accepted the rebuff. For several years after this we
hear nothing more of Greek expeditions to Italy, though
there may have been intrigues with the young Prince of
Benevento, who married a Greek wife named Wantia,
a relative of the Emperor, and in various ways showed
that he fretted under his galling vassalage to the
Frankish king.

But in Constantinople itself during these years of
truce with the West, strange and terrible events were
happening. The young Emperor Constantine VI. found
as he grew up to manhood that he was an absolute
cipher in his empire and in his palace. All power was
kept by Irene in her own hands, all orders went through
her confidential minister the eunuch Stauracius. To

these two all suppliants addressed their petitions. Constantine himself was treated as of no account to any
man. Brooding over the daily slights which he had to
endure, and resenting also, it is said, the manœuvre
which had deprived him of his fair young Frankish
bride, and tied him to the unloved and childless Armenian,
he began in 790 to look around for partisans who would
enable him to effect a revolution and become a real
instead of a puppet emperor. The plan of the conspirators (among whom were two patricians and the great
minister called *magister officiorum*), was to arrest the
empress, send her off to banishment in Sicily, and proclaim Constantine sole emperor. The ever watchful
Stauracius, however, obtained intelligence of the plot,
arrested the conspirators, ordered some of them to be
flogged, tonsured, and sent into the Sicilian exile which
they had planned for Irene ; the *magister officiorum* received some degrading punishment and was imprisoned
in his own house ; and lastly this same punishment of
seclusion was inflicted on Constantine, after his mother
had herself struck him and attacked him with an angry
woman's invective. Then a new and strange oath was
administered to all the soldiers in the capital and its
neighbourhood. " So long as thou livest, O Empress !
we will not suffer thy son to reign." These events took
place in the spring or summer of 791. In September
of that year there came a change. The soldiers who
were stationed in Armenia, when they were required to
take the new oath, refused. "We will not put the
name of Irene before that of Constantine," said they,
" but will swear obedience as of old to Constantine and
Irene." The disaffection spread ; the regiments which

had sworn the new oath to Irene forgot their vows
and joined the soldiers from Armenia. By the end of
October the revolution was complete. Irene was compelled by the clamour of the soldiers to liberate her son
from confinement; she was deprived of all power, and
Constantine was hailed as sole emperor. Stauracius
was beaten, tonsured and sent into exile in Armenia.
Aetius, another eunuch and confidant of Irene, was also
banished, and a clean sweep was made of all the menial
eunuch train, through whom apparently for ten years
the empire had been governed.

But, unfortunately, the character of the young
emperor, weakened by the subjection in which his
mother had kept him, was utterly inadequate to the
duties of his new position. With extraordinary folly,
after a few months he drew Irene forth from the seclusion of her palace, and allowed the people to shout once
more, "Long life to Constantine and Irene." He went
forth to war with the Bulgarians and was badly beaten.
This humiliation of the imperial arms caused the soldiers
in the city to plot for the elevation of Nicephorus, a
half-brother of Leo IV. and uncle of Constantine VI.
The young emperor arrested Nicephorus and ordered
him to be blinded; and at the same time the tongues
of four other of his uncles were cut out (792). These
barbarous punishments, blinding and mutilation, were
characteristic of the Constantinople of that day, but
the resort to them on so large a scale proved the alarm
as well as the cruelty of the young emperor, and must
have helped to lose him the hearts of his subjects. His
mother and Stauracius (who was now back again in the
palace) were thought to have counselled these cruel

deeds; and they certainly succeeded in embroiling him
with his old supporters, the Armenian soldiers, whose
revolts plunged the empire in civil war.

The climax of the emperor's unpopularity seems to
have been reached when (in January 795) he put away
his Armenian wife, compelling her to enter a convent,
and in September of the same year publicly celebrated
his union with a lady of her bedchamber named
Theodote. He had now lost the favour of the multitude, while his mother was ever at work forming a
party among the officers by promises and bribes,
suggesting that they should depose her son and
proclaim her sole empress. On the 14th of June
797 Constantine went, after witnessing an equestrian
performance in the circus, to worship in the church
of St. Mamas in the environs of Constantinople.
The conspirators, whose movements were directed by
Stauracius, endeavoured to seize him there, but he
seems to have been warned, and escaped in the imperial
boat to the Bithynian shore. Unhappily his mother's
friends and his own bitterest foes accompanied his
flight. There was hesitation and delay, and there
seemed a possibility that the soldiers would rally round
him and his cause might yet triumph. The ruthless
Irene sent a secret message to his adherents, "Unless
in some way or other you effect his capture I will
inform the emperor of all the plot which you and I
have formed against him." Fear made the conspirators
bold; they seized the emperor while at his prayers,
forced him to re-embark, and hurried him back across
the Sea of Marmora to Constantinople. There, after the
lapse of some weeks, in the Purple Chamber of the palace,

they put out his eyes, purposely performing the cruel operation with such brutality as to endanger his life. It was, in fact, supposed by many that he was dead, but he appears to have lingered on through many revolutions, an obscure and forgotten sufferer, for more than twenty years after his mutilation.

The deed was done on Saturday the 15th of August 797, at the ninth hour of the day. On the same day of the week and at the same hour, five years before, had his uncle suffered the same punishment. Men observed the coincidence and traced a divine retribution therein. But with greater horror did they learn that the emperor had suffered this brutal punishment in the Purple Chamber which was always reserved for the birth of an emperor's children. Here, in the very same room of the palace where he first saw the light, did he with the connivance, if not by the express command, of his mother lose the light of day and all that makes life worth living. "For seventeen days," says the historian, himself an image-worshipper and adherent of Irene, "the sun was darkened and did not give forth his rays, so that vessels lost their course and drifted helplessly, and all men said and confessed that because of the blinding of the emperor the sun did not show his beams. Thus did Irene his mother obtain supreme power."

The character of the Empress Irene receives unbounded praise from the writers of the image-worshipping party. She is for them "the most pious Irene," "that strong-minded and God-guided woman, if, indeed, it be right to call her a woman, who was armed against all foes and all calamities with truly masculine temper."

"Irene, that strong-minded and God-beloved woman, if we ought to call 'woman' one who surpassed even man in her pious disposition, one through whom God mercifully expelled the crooked heresy which had crept snakelike into the Church and brought back orthodoxy."

But neither these flatteries of the monkish image-worshippers, nor her outward show of magnificence when, on Easter Monday (799), the proud Athenian rode forth from the Church of the Apostles in a golden car drawn by four white horses, which were driven by four patricians, and showered money among the multitude after the fashion of the ancient Consuls of Rome, represented the real place of the empress in the hearts of her subjects. The rule of Irene meant, as every one knew, the rule and the bickerings of the eunuchs who advised her. Moreover, there was really no precedent for a woman sitting alone in the seat of empire. When Pulcheria, sister of Theodosius II., was hailed as Augusta, it was on condition of her giving her hand to the soldier Marcian. Theodora and Sophia were Augustæ, but ruled only during the lifetime of their husbands. When Martina, widow of Heraclius, tried to pose as joint-ruler with her son and stepson (641), the multitude shouted an indignant denial of her claims. "How can you sit upon the throne and answer foreign envoys when they come to the royal city. God forbid that the polity of the Romans should come into such a plight as that." It was a hundred and fifty-six years since the Byzantine populace had hurled these words at Martina and compelled her to descend from the throne, but we may be sure that the spirit which prompted them still dwelt in the hearts of the mass of the people who yet called themselves Romans. To be ruled by a woman, and such a woman, the despoiler and all but murderer of her own son, was felt to be an unendurable humiliation. The insecurity of Irene's position was shown by the shortness of her reign, but that short reign of five years (797-802) was long enough to include, in a certain sense to necessitate, the great event which will be the subject of the following chapter.

CHAPTER XI

CAROLUS AUGUSTUS

THE events described at the end of the last chapter happened in August 797. In the autumn of the following year, when Charles was resting at Aachen from the fatigues of a Saxon campaign on the banks of the Elbe, there appeared before him two Byzantine ambassadors, Michael, aforetime Patrician of Phrygia, and Theophilus, a priest of Blachernæ, who, on behalf of the Empress Irene, sought for and obtained the restoration of friendly relations between the empire and the kingdom. The covenant of peace was ratified by the return of an illustrious Greek captive, Sisinnius, brother of the Patriarch Tarasius, who had been taken prisoner probably in the Apulian war of 788.

But a far more distinguished visitor than either Michael or Theophilus was to visit Charles's court in the following year, and to plead in lowlier fashion for his help. To understand the nature of this visit we must go back for a few years and glance at the events which had been happening not in the New, but in the Old Rome.

On the day after Christmas Day, 795, died Pope

Hadrian I. after a long and eventful pontificate. The relations between him and Charles had not been always friendly, for Hadrian had found that no more than the Lombard king would the Frank grant the exorbitant demands for towns and lordships which were unceasingly urged in the name of St. Peter. Still there had been a certain similarity of spirit and temper which had drawn these two strong men together, and, as we have already seen, Charles mourned for the death of Hadrian as if he had been the dearest of his sons.

On the death of Hadrian, Leo III. was immediately elected to the papal throne. He was a Roman by birth, an inmate from his childhood of the Lateran palace, and had gone through the regular gradation of ecclesiastical offices till he had reached the high position of papal *vestararius*. It would seem probable that he was the candidate most acceptable to the clerics of the Roman Church, though the result showed that there was a large party among the great lay-officers of the papal court to whom his elevation was by no means welcome. He was, at a crisis of his fortunes, accused by bitter enemies of adultery and forgery, but no proof was offered of these charges, and there seems no reason to believe that his moral character was not stainless. There are some indications, however, that he was not loved by the people of Rome. Possibly his temper may have been harsh : possibly too they were beginning to chafe under the yoke of the dignitary who but lately was their spiritual pastor, sometimes their champion, but who now asserted himself as their sovereign.

Immediately on his elevation, Pope Leo sent

messengers to Charles announcing his election and carrying to him the keys of St. Peter's tomb and the banner
of the city of Rome. This act of submission to the
great Patrician of Rome, to whom the pope looked for
confirmation of his rights and protection from his
enemies, was represented in the celebrated mosaic in
the Triclinium of the Lateran palace, of which a toler-
ably accurate seventeenth-century copy still exists on
the outside wall of the oratory called the *Sancta
Sanctorum*, immediately in front of the Lateran. In it
the Apostle Peter, of colossal size, is represented sitting
with the keys on his lap. Before him, on his right,
kneels Pope Leo, to whom he is giving the *pallium ;*
on his left "our lord Carulus," to whom he gives a
banner ; and underneath is an inscription in barbarous
Latin stating that the blessed Peter gives life to Pope
Leo and victory to King Charles. Charles is represented as wearing a moustache, but no beard. He has
a broad pleasant face and is crowned with a conical
diadem.

The Frankish king replied to the new pope by
sending to him his friend and chaplain Angilbert,
bearing a letter in which he dilated on the various
duties which Providence had assigned to its sender and
its receiver. "It is ours with the help of the divine
piety externally to defend the Holy Church of Christ by
our arms from all pagan inroads and infidel devastation,
and internally to fortify it by the recognition of the
Catholic faith. It is yours, most holy father, with
hands raised to God like Moses, to help our warfare ;
that by your intercession the Christian people may everywhere have the victory over its enemies, and the name

of our Lord Jesus Christ may be magnified throughout
the whole world." At the same time Angilbert brought
the share of the Avar booty which Charles had set
aside for Hadrian, but which came too late to gladden
the heart of the aged pontiff.

This exchange of embassies took place in 796. Two
years later the Christian world was horrified by the
news of a brutal outrage enacted in the streets of Rome.
On the 25th of April 798, the pope was mounted and
preparing to ride forth from Rome along the Flaminian
Way, in order to celebrate what was called the Greater
Litany, a religious function which had taken the place
of the heathen *Robigalia* and in which the Divine protection was implored for the springing corn against the
perils of blasting and mildew. Suddenly, ere he had
emerged from the city, he was set upon by a band of
ruffians who had been lying in wait at the church of St.
Silvestro in Capite, on the right hand of the Corso.
They tore him from his horse, they belaboured him
with cudgels ; according to one account they tried to
practise upon him the Byzantine atrocities of pulling
out the eyes and cutting out the tongue ; at any rate
they left him speechless and helpless in the solitary
street, for all his long train of attendants, as well as the
crowd which had gathered after him to go forth in
bright procession along the Flaminian Way, forsook
him and fled.

There is some reason to suppose that this attack was
an outburst of civic fury, exasperated by some acts of
the unpopular pontiff; but there is no doubt that the
movement was directed by two men, Paschalis and
Campulus, who were high in office in the papal house-

hold, and one or both of whom were nephews of the pope's predecessor Hadrian. A lurid light is shed by this fact on the heart-burnings and angry disappointments which were often caused among the clients of a deceased pope by the election of his successor.

After suffering many indignities the unhappy Leo was dragged at night to the monastery of St. Erasmus on the Cœlian hill. Here he was closely confined for some days, but he recovered somewhat from his bruises, and sight returned—miraculously the next generation said —to his injured eyes. By the help of a faithful servant, his chamberlain Albinus, he succeeded in escaping— probably by a rope—down the wall of the convent, and was taken by his friends to St. Peter's. Here he was soon in perfect safety, for the Frankish duke of Spoleto, Winighis, who had heard of the murderous assault, came with an army to his rescue and escorted him to his own city, a safe stronghold among the mountains of Umbria. The foiled conspirators, who had heard with terror of their victim's flight, vented their rage on the house of Albinus, which they gave to the flames. Probably for many subsequent months anarchy ruled in Rome.

In the disturbed state of Italy, and with Rome given over to his unscrupulous foes, the only resource left for the pope was in the protection of Charles; and to his court, or rather to his camp, for he was immersed in the Saxon war, Leo III. repaired in the summer of 799. It was now more than forty-five years since a pope (Stephen II.) had crossed the Alps on a similar errand. Much had happened in the interval. The monarchy of the "most unspeakable" Lombards had been overthrown; the successor of St. Peter had become one of the great

princes of the earth ; and yet, as Leo must with sadness
have reflected, not even sovereignty had brought safety.
"Wounded in the house of his friends," the Bishop of
Rome had received from the hands of his own courtiers
and subjects treatment infinitely more cruel and contu-
melious than any that the much vituperated Lombard
had ever inflicted on his predecessors.   Musing on these
things Pope Leo doubtless saw that the day-dream of a
papal sovereignty extending over all Italy could not be
realised.   Rather must he make his Frankish friend and
protector stronger in Italy.   The Patrician of Rome must
take some higher and more imposing title, and must be
induced to give more assiduous attention to the affairs
of the Italian peninsula.

As in that earlier papal visit Charles, then a lad of
twelve, had been sent to meet Stephen II., so now did
Charles send his son Pippin (a young man of twenty-two,
and the crowned king of Italy) to meet Pope Leo.
Pippin escorted the venerable guest into his father's
presence.   Pope and king embraced and kissed with
tears.   The clergy in the papal train intoned the *Gloria
in Excelsis*, and the nobles and courtiers round added
their joyful acclamations.   This meeting took place at
Paderborn, where Charles had built a new and splendid
church in the place of the edifice often destroyed by the
Saxons.   In this church Pope Leo hallowed an altar,
which he enriched with relics of the protomartyr Stephen
brought by him from Rome, and assured the king that
by the powerful intercession of that saint the church
would be preserved from future devastation.

Leo remained probably for about two months, from
July to September, at Paderborn, in constant inter-

course with Charles.   Much would doubtless be said in
the conferences between the two potentates concerning
the condition of the Church, the heresy of the Adoptians,
the Iconoclastic controversy, and above all concerning
the charges brought against the pope's character by his
relentless enemies in Rome.   Was there also something
said about that great event towards which, as we know,
the course of history was tending, the bestowal of the
imperial title on Charles ?   Here we have only conjectures to guide us, but in these conjectures we must take
account of one most powerful influence upon which I
have hitherto been silent, the influence of the absent, but
continually consulted Northumbrian, Alcuin.

Alcuin, born of a noble Anglian family about the year
735, and therefore some seven years older than Charles,
was brought up from childhood in the monastic seminary
of York, and there drank in with eager lips the learning,
deepest and best of its day in all Europe, which that
celebrated school imparted to its pupils.   Bede, it is
true, had died about the time of Alcuin's birth, but
from Bede's pupil Ecgbert, Archbishop of York (732-766),
and from his successor Ælbert (767-778), he acquired a
knowledge, not only of theology, but also of many secular
arts and sciences.   To astronomy he was led by the
intricate calculations and endless discussions concerning
the true date of Easter.   But in the archiepiscopal
library, as Alcuin himself tells us, there was also a respectable collection of the Latin classics, Pliny, Cicero,
Virgil, Lucan, Statius are all enumerated by him, as
well as Aristotle, who was probably represented only by
a Latin translation.   To the study of these authors the
young Northumbrian gave many industrious years;

Virgil especially was long the master of his soul, and
the legends of a later generation told how the visit of
an evil spirit to his cell was necessary to frighten him
away from the nocturnal study of the Mantuan bard into
the repetition of the Psalms appointed for the midnight
service.   Certain it is, however, that he did not forsake
the study of the profane authors, until they had thoroughly
permeated his style.   Although an ecclesiastic he wrote
Latin, both prose and verse, of which no Roman in the
first century need have been ashamed.   To pass from
the continual barbarisms, obscurities, puerilities of
Gregory of Tours, of Fredegarius, or even of the authors
of the *Liber Pontificalis*, to the easily flowing prose, or
hexameter verse of Alcuin is like going from the ill-spelt
productions of a half-educated ploughman to the letters
of Cowper or the poetry of Goldsmith.

Alcuin has been called the Erasmus of the eighth century, and though in one respect the comparison is too
flattering, since the Northumbrian did but little for
critical science, it gives on the whole not an incorrect
impression of the literary position of this man, the
"child and champion" of the Carolingian Renascence.
It is evident that he and the men with whom he associated, Angles, Saxons, or Franks, were tired of the
barbarism which had pervaded Europe for three centuries,
and looked back with longing, perhaps sometimes with
unwise longing, to the great days of Roman supremacy
and peace.   Even their Teutonic names were to them
somewhat of a humiliation.   In the literary circle or
academy which formed itself in Charles's court, chiefly
under Alcuin's influence, the members assumed classical
names (like the Melancthon and Œcolampadius of a later

Renascence), and corresponded with one another under these disguises. Thus Alcuin himself was Flaccus Albinus, Riçulf (afterwards Archbishop of Mainz) was Damœtas ; Angilbert, Charles's chaplain, was Homer ; Arno, Archbishop of Salzburg, was Aquila. The name of the great king himself was David, a name admirably chosen to express his piety, his success in war, and his love of women.

The event which brought " Albinus " and his " dearest David " together was a journey which Alcuin undertook to Rome in 781, in order to obtain the *pallium* for his .friend and superior, Eanbald II., Archbishop of York. Alcuin himself was at this time, and in fact throughout middle life and old age, only a deacon, though from his learning and piety he wielded more influence than many bishops. Returning from Rome, he met Charles at Parma, and was entreated by him to return to Frankland on the accomplishment of his mission. He protested that he could only do this with the consent of his king and his archbishop, and these consents having been obtained he returned to Charles's court and resided there, a sort of literary prime minister, from 782 to 796, with the exception of a visit to his own country between 790 and 792. Though apparently he never entered the monastic state, he received from Charles, as a piece of preferment, the headship of two abbeys, that of Bethlehem at Ferrières and that of St. Lupus at Troyes. In 796, feeling the need of repose, he obtained his master's reluctant permission to retire to the great monastery of St. Martin at Tours, which was placed under his rule, and where he spent the remainder of his days. This absence from the court is a fortunate thing for us, for to it we owe the letters between Charles and Alcuin, of which a considerable number are still preserved, and which show both king and deacon in no unpleasing light. Sometimes Alcuin advises the king to treat the conquered Saxons and Avars tenderly, and not to gall them with the yoke of tithes. Sometimes he explains to his royal friend the meaning of the terms Septuagesima and Sexagesima. Then he enters into long discussions about the calendar, the date of Easter, the intercalations necessary to bring the solar and the lunar years into harmony. The king half mischievously refers these calculations to the well-taught pages of his palace, who discover in them some errors, which, after much mutual banter, the elder scholar is compelled to acknowledge. Always, however, the intercourse is friendly, sincere, elevating. The king does not patronise, and the deacon does not cringe. One cannot but feel in reading these letters that both men were made to be loved.

Such was the man who, as there is every reason to believe, had whispered to many of his friends the fateful word "Imperator" before Pope Leo III. arrived, a hunted and half-blinded fugitive, at Charles's court.

In the month of May (799) Alcuin had written to his royal master a remarkable letter, commenting on the tidings which Charles had sent him of the assault on Pope Leo. From this letter it will be well to extract some sentences.

"To his peace-making lord King David, Albinus wishes health. I thank your Goodness, sweetest David, for remembering my littleness and making me acquainted with the facts which your faithful servant has brought to my ears. Were I present with you I should have many counsels to offer to your Dignity, if you had opportunity to listen or I eloquence to speak. For I love to write concerning your prosperity, the stability of the kingdom given you by God and the advancement of the Holy Church of Christ. All which are much troubled and stained by the daring deeds of wicked men which have been perpetrated, not on obscure and ignoble persons, but on the greatest and the highest.

"For there have been hitherto three persons higher than all others in this world. One is the Apostolic Sublimity who rules by vicarious power from the seat of St. Peter, prince of the apostles. And what has been done to him, who was the ruler of the aforesaid see, you have in your goodness informed me.

"The second is the Imperial dignity and power of the second Rome. How impiously the governor of that empire [Constantine VI.] has been deposed, not by aliens but by his own people and fellow citizens, universal rumour tells us.

"The third is the royal dignity in which the decree of our Lord Jesus Christ has placed you as ruler of the Christian people, more excellent in power than the other aforesaid dignities, more illustrious in wisdom, more sublime in the dignity of your kingdom. Lo! now on you alone the salvation of the churches of Christ falls and rests. You are the avenger of crimes, the guide of the wanderers, the comforter of the mourners, the exalter of the good.

"Have not the most frightful examples of wickedness now made themselves manifest in the Roman see where of old there was the brightest religion and piety? These men, blinded in their own hearts, have blinded him who was their true head. There is in that place no fear of God, no wisdom, no charity. What good thing can you look for where these are absent? These are the perilous times long since foretold by Him who was Himself the Truth, and therefore the love of many waxes cold."

Alcuin then advises his royal friend to make peace if possible with the "unutterable" people (the Saxons), to forbear threats in dealing with them and to intermit, at any rate for a time, the exaction of tithes. Evidently this prudent counsellor felt that the affairs of Italy had now the most pressing claim on his master's attention, and that it would be wise to concentrate all his forces for the solution of the problem which there awaited him.

It was then to a monarch thus prepossessed in his favour by the representations of one of his nearest friends that Leo III. appealed in the interview at Paderborn. The pope's accusers sent their representatives to the Saxon towns, repeating the charges of adultery and perjury, and claiming that the pope should be called upon to deny the truth of these charges on oath. Privily they gave him the advice of professed well-wishers that he should give up the contest, lay down his papal dignity and retire in peace to some convent. But the king, while reserving the investigation into these charges for some future assembly to be held in Rome, showed by his conduct that he attached to them but little importance. After several weeks' sojourn at Paderborn, Leo was dismissed with all honour from the camp and was escorted by royal *missi* reverently back to Rome, where he received an enthusiastic welcome from his penitent subjects (30th November 799).

The close of this year was saddened by the tidings of the death of those two brave champions of Frankish civilisation, Gerold and Eric. In the spring of 800, Charles set forth on an expedition into Neustria, a part of his dominions which he had apparently not visited for two-and-twenty years. Piratical raids of the Northmen seem to have been the determining cause of this expedition, the object of which was to put the coast of the Channel in a proper state of defence. He also, however, received the submission of some Breton chiefs who had long been in a chronic condition of revolt; he made the round of his villas and country palaces in Neustria; and above all he visited the tomb of St. Martin at Tours, and had a long spell of close and confidential intercourse with his friend Alcuin. Here at Tours his fifth and last wife Liutgard died (4th June 800), and her illness probably lengthened his stay in that city. At length, after revisiting Rhine-land and holding a *placitum* at Mainz (August 800) he began his last and most celebrated journey into Italy.

Having rested for seven days at Ravenna, where he probably inhabited the palace built by Theodoric wherein the Byzantine exarch had dwelt, he marched down the coast of the Adriatic to Ancona. From thence he despatched his son Pippin to lay waste the territories of that unruly vassal, Grimwald of Benevento. Charles himself proceeded through the Picene and Sabine districts by the old *Via Salaria*, and arrived at Nomentum, fourteen miles from Rome. Here he was met by the pope, who accosted him with every show of humility and deference. Pope and king supped together at Nomentum, and then Leo returned to arrange for the triumphal entry into Rome. Next day (24th November 800) this great pageant was enacted. The banners of the city of Rome borne by citizens, the gilt crosses borne by ecclesiastics, came in long procession to meet the great Patrician. Groups of citizens and of the foreigners resident in Rome, Franks, Frisians, Saxons (among the latter doubtless many of our own countrymen), stationed at intervals along the Salarian Way, thundered forth their *laudes* as the king rode by. St. Peter's Church, now as before, was the goal of his pilgrimage, and on the broad marble stairs stood the pope, with all his train of bishops and clergy, to welcome him. He sprang from his horse, mounted the steps (not now apparently on his knees), and after receiving the papal blessing went in and paid his devotions at the tomb of St. Peter.

The chief business which had brought King Charles to Rome was, of course, the enquiry into the brutal assault on the pope and the clearing of his character from the charges brought against him. Already the Frankish *missi* who accompanied Leo to Rome had held a preliminary enquiry, the result of which was that Paschalis and Campulus had been sent across the Alps to Charles for judgment. Now apparently they returned in his train, not so much to defend themselves on the score of the outrage (for their guilt was too clear) as to prove, if they could, their often-repeated accusations. A great synod was assembled at St. Peter's on the 1st of December, and was opened by a speech from the king. According to the papal biographer, the ecclesiastics composing the synod all with one accord declared :

"We do not dare to judge the Apostolic see, which is the head of all the Church of God ; for by it and by the Apostle's vicar we all are judged, but the see itself is judged of no man, and this has been the custom from old time." Whether this high papal doctrine was proclaimed and accepted or not, it certainly seems as if Paschalis and Campulus entirely failed to make good their charges ; but the pope offered, if his conduct were not drawn into a precedent against his successors, to accept the challenge to clear himself by oath from the charges brought against him. It is possible that the pope was only slowly brought to make this concession, for it was not till more than three weeks after the assembling of the synod that the next step was taken. On the 23rd of December, in the presence of the Roman clergy, as well as of the Frankish followers of the king, Pope Leo appeared in the *ambo* of St. Peter's, bearing a copy of the four gospels, which he clasped to his breast, and then he swore with a loud and clear voice : "Of all those charges which the Romans, my unjust persecutors, have brought against me, I declare in the presence of God and St. Peter, in whose church I stand, that I am innocent, since I have neither done those things whereof I am accused nor procured the doing of them."

The result of the whole investigation was that Paschalis and Campulus and their accomplices were found guilty of high treason and condemned to death, a sentence which, on the intercession of the pope, was commuted to perpetual banishment into Frank-land.

During the weeks that the papal trial was proceeding Charles, of course, abode in Rome, whether in one of the old imperial dwellings on the Palatine, or as an honoured

guest of the pope at the Lateran we are not informed.
It was observed that now, as on the occasion of a
previous visit to Rome, out of courtesy to the pope he
laid aside his Frankish dress—a tunic with silver border,
a vest of otterskins and sable, and a blue cloak—and
wore instead, after the Roman fashion, a long tunic and
a *chlamys* over it, shoes also made like those of the
Romans, instead of his Frankish boots with stockings
and garters.

It was precisely during this month of December that
by a fortunate coincidence, the priest Zacharias, whom
more than a year before Charles had sent on a mission to
the holy places, returned from the East. Two monks
came with him, from Olivet and St. Saba, sent by the
Patriarch of Jerusalem, and bringing by way of blessing
from that ecclesiastic the keys of the Holy Sepulchre
and of Calvary, of Jerusalem and Mount Zion, together
with a consecrated banner. A more striking testimony
to the world-wide fame of the Frankish conqueror could
hardly have been rendered than this, which must have
been meant to invest Charles with a kind of protectorate
over the most sacred sites in Christendom.

The pope's solemn oath of self-exculpation was sworn
on the 23rd of December. Two days later was transacted that yet more solemn ceremony by which the
Patriarch of the Western Church, thus purged from the
stains which his assailants had sought to cast upon his
character, bestowed upon his royal champion that title
which set him highest among the rulers of the Christian
world. The scene was again laid in the great basilica
of St. Peter, a building, of course, utterly unlike to the
vast Renaissance temple of Bramante and Michael

Angelo. There, on Christmas morning, Charles the Frank was worshipping before the *Confessio* or tomb of St. Peter. The stately Roman *chlamys* hung around his shoulders; the crowd that filled the basilica could see with satisfaction the dainty Roman buskins of the kneeling monarch. When he rose from prayer Pope Leo approached him, placed upon his head a costly golden crown, and clothed him in the purple mantle of empire. "Then," says the papal biographer, "all the faithful Romans, beholding so great a champion given them, and knowing the love which he bare to the Holy Roman Church and its vicar, in obedience to the will of God and of St. Peter, the key-bearer of the kingdom of heaven, cried out with deep accordant voices : 'To Charles, most pious and august, crówned by God, the great and peace-bringing emperor, be life and victory!'" Thereupon the people sang their jubilant *laudes*, and the pope performed that lowly adoration wherewith his predecessors had been wont to greet a Valentinian or a Theodosius.

The deed was done, and the Holy Roman Empire, which lasted a thousand years, and only in the days of our fathers was shattered by the fist of Napoleon, was established, or (as Alcuin and Leo would have said) was re-established in Europe. It was a revolution, no doubt, that was enacted on that morning of the 25th of December 800. It could not have been justified out of the Digest or the Code. According to all the maxims of legitimacy which had prevailed for many preceding centuries, Charles was an usurper and Leo an inter-meddling traitor. And yet, if one could go back still earlier to the first days of the empire, the bestowal of the imperial title on Charles was not so utterly lawless a proceeding. The Roman Imperator in those early centuries was not by any elaborate process elected, but was always acclaimed. Acclaimed by the army, it is true, but also by the people, and there were doubtless many soldiers of the *militia cohortalis* of Rome present among the crowd who shouted for life and victory to the peace-bringing emperor. When acclaimed by army and people the Cæsar was, or ought to be, accepted by the Senate; and there are some indications that after centuries of suspended animation a body calling itself the Senate was at this time existing in Rome and consenting to the elevation of Charles. And these bodies, Senate, people, army, however insignificant in themselves, were at any rate Roman: they belonged to the true old Rome; they trod the forum of the republic, and looked up to the Palatine of the emperors; they were not like the bastard Romans of the Bosphorus, who chattered in Greek and wore the robes of Asia, but who had usurped for so many centuries the profitable trade-mark of the Senate and People of Rome. So, though there was but one precedent—and that the bad one of Maximin the Thracian—for conferring the dignity of emperor on a man of purely Teutonic descent, and though it is quite impossible to find a place for the chief actor, the Bishop of Rome, in the drama as played by all the earlier Cæsars, we may on the whole conclude that Charles became Roman Emperor by as good a title as any who had worn the purple since the days of Theodosius.

What were the chief causes which led to this great change in the political constitution of Europe? They have been already hinted at, and we shall probably not be wrong in enumerating them as follows.

First.—The great revival of classical learning, due chiefly to the labours of Anglo-Saxon scholars; a movement of which men like Bede and Alcuin were the standard-bearers. The minds which were influenced by this revival perceived plainly that the interests of civilisation, and to a certain extent of Christianity, had been in past centuries identical with those of the great Roman Empire; and from a genuine revival of that Empire (not from a mere ephemeral reconquest of certain cities or provinces by a *spatharius* or *cubicularius* setting sail from Constantinople), they anticipated, not altogether erroneously, great gains for the civilisation and the Christianity of the future.

Second.—The anomalous position of that which called itself the empire, which for the first time in its history found itself under what John Knox called "the monstrous regiment of a woman," and that woman the murderess of her child.

Third.—The brutal attack on Pope Leo made by the disappointed kinsmen of his predecessor. This event may well have produced an important change in the attitude of the pope towards the question of reviving the empire in the west. Before that day of April when he was assaulted by his own courtiers and left half dead in the streets of Rome, he may (as has been already hinted) have looked forward to a time when he should reign over the best part of Italy, subject to no king or governor; and when whispers reached him of the use of · the words "Emperor" and "Imperial" by the learned ecclesiastics of Charles's court he may in that mood of mind have shown that their proposals were little to his taste. After that fatal day, his reluctance, if he had any, to see one man in the Italian peninsula holding an indisputably higher position than his own, was changed into eager acquiescence in the scheme. He was willing, nay anxious, to see the purple robe encircling the stalwart limbs of the Frankish conqueror, if only he himself might take shelter under that robe from the dagger of the assassin.

In all this it may be truly said that we have failed to consider one important factor in the problem, the desires and ambitions of Charles himself. Unfortunately a mystery which we cannot penetrate hangs over that very subject. · One of his most intimate friends, his secretary Einhard, expressly says that Charles "at first so greatly disliked the title of Emperor and Augustus that he declared that if he could have known beforehand the intention of the pope he would never have entered the church on that day, though it was one of the holiest festivals of the year."

It used to be assumed that this reluctance on the part of Charles to receive the new dignity was only a bit of well-played comedy between him and Leo, that the Frankish king had been long aspiring to the imperial dignity, and had even put constraint upon the pope to force him to take part in the coronation. More recent discussion has shaken our confidence in this easy solution of the problem: and probably the greater number of writers on the history of this period now hold that Charles was speaking the truth when he expressed his dissatisfaction with the pope's proceedings. The cause of that dissatisfaction can only be conjectured. Einhard seems to hint that it was fear of the resentment of the Byzantine Cæsars, but this hardly seems a sufficient cause to one who remembers the low estate of the eastern monarchy under Irene.

With much more probability Professor Dahn argues that what Charles disliked was not the bestowal of the title in itself but its bestowal by the pope. He thinks that Charles and his counsellors had already, in 799, virtually resolved on the revival of the empire, that the pope penetrated their design, and determined that if that step were taken he at least would be chief actor in the drama; that by his adroit tactics he, so to speak, forced Charles's hand, and that the latter, foreseeing the evil consequences which would result from the precedent thus established, of a pope-crowned emperor, expressed his genuine feelings of vexation to his friend Einhard when he said, "Would that I had never entered St. Peter's on Christmas Day." Certainly the remembrance of all the miserable complications caused during the Middle Ages by the pope's claim to set the crown on the head of the emperor would do much to justify the unwillingness of a statesman such as the Frankish king to bind this chain round the limbs of his successors.

But even beyond this it seems possible that Charles's own mind was not fully made up as to the expediency of accepting the imperial diadem, by whomsoever bestowed. That the plan had been discussed (perhaps often discussed, through many years), by his more highly educated courtiers, cannot be denied. He may have been dazzled by the brilliancy of the position which was thus offered him; and yet the calmer judgment of that foreseeing mind of his may not have been satisfied that it was altogether wise for him to accept it. The Frankish kingdom, as it had been built up by the valour and patience of Charles and his forefathers, was a splendid and solid reality. This restored empire of Rome that they talked of, would be even more splendid, but would it be equally substantial? After all, the whole Roman *Orbis Terrarum* was not subject to his sway. Was it wise to assume a title which seemed to assert a shadowy claim to vast unsubdued territories? Was it wise to claim for a Teuton king that all-embracing authority wherewith the legists had invested the Roman Imperator? The controversies of Guelphs and Ghibellines, which distracted Italy for centuries, show that these questions, if they presented themselves to the mind of Charles, were questions which greatly needed an answer. And there was also a difficulty, which has perhaps not been sufficiently dwelt upon, arising from Charles's prospective division of his dominions among his sons. Charles, the eldest, was to succeed him in that Austrasian region which was the heart and stronghold of his kingdom. If any son were to inherit the Imperial dignity, sitting on a higher throne than his brethren and holding a certain pre-eminence over them, that son must be Charles. Yet Pippin, the second son, was the actual king and destined heir of Italy, and would rule over Rome, the city from which the Roman Emperor was to take his title. Here was the germ of probable future embroilments between his sons, such as the prudent Charles may well have feared to foster.

Upon the whole, therefore, it appears a probable conclusion that Charles, though he accepted the imperial crown, accepted it with genuine reluctance, and that he was the passive approver rather than the active and ambitious contriver of the great revolution of 800.

In the summer of 801 Charles recrossed the Alps to his home in Rhine-land. In the thirteen years of life which remained to him he never again entered Italy, but he was, during the greater part of that time, well represented there by his son, the able and courageous Pippin.

A question which doubtless excited much interest in all the Frankish world was, how Charles's assumption of the imperial title would be viewed at Constantinople. There must have been many among the Byzantine statesmen who bitterly resented it, but Irene's position was too insecure to permit of her giving utterance to their indignation. It is indeed stated by a Greek chronicler that Charles sent an embassy to Constantinople proposing to unite the two empires by his own marriage with Irene, and that the project was only foiled by the opposition of the eunuch Aetius who was scheming to secure the succession for his brother. Whether this be true or not (and the entire silence of the Frankish authorities on the subject is somewhat suspicious), there is no doubt that a friendly embassy from Irene appeared at Charles's court in 802, and was replied to by a return embassy, consisting of Bishop Jesse and Count Helmgaud, who were despatched from Aachen in the same year, and that this embassy may have carried a declaration of love from the elderly Frank to the middle-aged Athenian. But not in such romantic fashion was the reconciliation of the two empires to be effected. While the bishop and the count were tarrying at Constantinople they were the unwilling spectators of a palace-revolution, which possibly may have been hastened by their presence and by the fear of a treaty, wounding to the national pride. On the 31st October 802, Irene was deposed and the Grand Treasurer of the empire, Nicephorus, was raised to the throne. Irene's life was spared, but she was banished to an island in the Sea of Marmora, and afterwards to the isle of Lesbos, where according to one account she was so meanly supplied with the necessaries of life by her penurious successor, that this proud and brilliant lady had to support herself by spinning. She died on the 9th August 803.

Again the precariousness of the new ruler's position compelled him to assume a courteous tone towards the Frankish sovereign. Charles's ambassadors were accompanied on their return journey by three envoys from Nicephorus, a bishop, an abbot, and a life-guardsman, who were charged with many professions of amity and good-will to the Frankish king. In all this, however, there was no sign of recognition of Charles as Emperor, and for any such recognition Charles apparently waited for eight years in vain.

In 806 there was actual war between the two states, the bone of contention being the little island-state of Venice, which was now rising into commercial importance and in whose obscure and entangled history two parties, a Frankish and a Byzantine, are dimly discernible. After a long time a fleet from Constantinople appeared for a second time in Venetian waters, but was not able to prevent the victory of Pippin, who made a grand attack by land and sea, and subdued apparently the cities of the lagunes, whose capital was at this time shifted to the Rialto. This occurred in 810, but in the same year there appeared at Aachen an ambassador from Nicephorus who probably, amid the usual unmeaning professions of friendship, conveyed a hint that his master might be willing, for a suitable compensation, to recognise Charles as Roman Emperor. On this hint, for which he had waited with statesmanlike patience, the Frankish monarch acted. He expressed his willingness to surrender the Adriatic territories, Venetia, Istria, Liburnia, and Dalmatia to "his brother Nicephorus" and sent Heito, Bishop of Basel, with two colleagues to settle the terms of the new treaty.

Unhappily, when Heito and his colleagues arrived in Constantinople they found a change in the occupant of the palace. Nicephorus had fallen in battle, a most disastrous battle, with Krum, the King of the Bulgarians (25th July 811); but his brother-in-law and successor, Michael Rhangabé, was abundantly willing to confirm the proposed accommodation with the most powerful sovereign of the west. In truth the suggestion must have come at a most welcome season, for Constantinople was just then as hard pressed by the Bulgarian as she had ever been by the Avar or the Saracen. So it came to pass that yet another embassy from the Byzantine court appeared at Aachen in January 812. A formal document containing the terms of the treaty of peace was handed to them by Charles in the church of the Virgin, and possibly the counterpart was received from the ambassadors. But the essential point was, that they sang a litany in the Greek tongue in which they hailed the Frankish sovereign as Imperator and Basileus. That was a formal recognition of Charles's equality, and thenceforth no one could doubt that there was an Emperor by the Rhine as well as by the Bosphorus.

CHAPTER XII

OLD AGE

THE somewhat tedious tale of the wars of the August and Pacific Emperor is happily almost at an end.

We hear of repeated ravages by Scandinavian pirates along the shores of the German and Atlantic oceans: by Moorish pirates along the shore of the Mediterranean: and with neither class of freebooters does Charles appear to have grappled very successfully, for the good reason that he never devoted a sufficient portion of his energies to the establishment of a navy. The well-known story that Charles saw from the windows of his palace at Narbonne the Danish sea-rovers scudding over the waters of the Gulf of Lyons, and foretold with tears the miseries which these freebooters should bring upon his posterity and their realm, comes to us on the late and doubtful authority of the Monk of St. Gall and need not be accepted as authentic history : but that was one of the thunderclouds looming up on the horizon of the ninth century whether Charles was ware of it or no. While the pirate barks of the Scandinavians were spreading terror over the islands of the west, the land forces of the King of Denmark were threatening the north-eastern boundary of Charles's kingdom. Here the Saxons, at last subdued into loyalty, were, as we have seen, bounded on the east by the Sclavonic nations, the Abodrites, and the Wiltzi, and on the north, in Sleswik, by the Danes. The usual arrangement of parties in the perpetually recurring frontier wars was this: the Saxons (that is the Frankish kingdom) in alliance with the Abodrites on one side, and the Danes with the Wiltzi on the other. The king of the Abodrites was named Drasko; the king of the Danes was Godofrid, a proud, high-soaring king of pirates, who ventured to put himself on an equality with the mighty Frankish Emperor, declaring that Friesland and Saxonland were of right his territories, and that he would appear one day with all his warriors round him at Aachen and would try conclusions with Charles.

It was in the years from 808 to 810 that this menace to the tranquillity of the Frankish kingdom showed itself in its most alarming shape. In the first of those years Godofrid invaded the territory of the Abodrites and ravaged their lands. Drasko fled before him, but another chieftain, Godelaib, was treacherously taken and hung. The Wiltzi joined forces with the Danes: and after much slaughter on both sides (for the flower of the Danish nobility fell in this campaign), the Abodrites were made subject to tribute to the Danish king. In retaliation for this onslaught on a friendly tribe, the younger Charles was sent across the Elbe with an army, but though he ravaged the lands of some Sclavonic allies of the Danes he seems to have returned home without achieving any decisive victory. Then both the two chief powers, knowing that a war of reprisals was imminent, took to fortifying their frontier. Godofrid drew across Holstein that line of forts which has since become famous as the Dannewerk, and Charles erected fortresses on his side of the border, especially restoring the stronghold of Hohbuoki which had been destroyed by the Wiltzi.

Next year (809) Godofrid sought and obtained an interview with Charles at Badenfliot (in Holstein), desiring to exculpate himself from the charge of having provoked the previous war. But the interview came to nothing. The Danish king did not sincerely desire peace, and probably showed too plainly the arrogance of his ignorant soul and his foolish pretensions to equality with Charles. He succeeded, however, in patching up a temporary peace with the Abodrite chief Drasko who returned to his own land, but only to fall a victim some months later to the treacherous attack of a vassal of Godofrid's, who was believed to have been incited to the deed by the Danish king. In 810 the contest seemed to be growing desperate, and the wild hopes of Godofrid to be approaching fulfilment. A fleet of two hundred Danish ships sailed to Friesland, laid waste all the multitudinous islands on the Frisian shore, and landed an army on the mainland, which defeated the Frisians in three pitched battles and laid upon them a tribute, of which 100 lbs. of silver had been already paid when tidings of the disaster reached the emperor in his palace at Aachen. He at once set about the too long delayed construction of a fleet: and at the mouths of all the rivers which poured into the German Ocean, the Channel, and the Atlantic, the sound of the ship-builder's hammer was heard. Then in the midst of his anxieties he received two welcome pieces of intelligence. The first was that the Danish fleet had returned home : the second that Godofrid was dead, murdered by one of his vassals, a fitting retribution for the assassination of Drasko, which he himself had instigated.

After this there was peace for the rest of Charles's life between him and the Danes. Hemming, the nephew and successor of Godofrid, was not strong enough to continue the aggressive policy of his uncle, and on Hemming's death (812) there was a bloody civil war between his family and the rival dynasty of Harald. However, Charles wisely did not relax his naval prepara- tions, but in the year 811 repaired to Boulogne in order to review the fleet which he had commanded to be assembled there from the various estuaries of his kingdom. Was it partly in remembrance of this event, that nearly a thousand years later, Napoleon, that great imitator of Charlemagne, caused his flotilla to assemble at Boulogne for the long meditated, never accomplished, invasion of Britain ?

The last years of the great emperor's life were saddened by a succession of domestic afflictions : but before describing them it will be well to give a glance at his family life in his happier middle age before these troubles fell upon him. As we have seen, Charles was five times married. Of his first wife Himiltrud, mother of the hunchback Pippin, we know nothing, save that, according to Pope Stephen's account, she was " sprung from the very noble race of the Franks," and that she must have either died or been divorced before 770, when he married the daughter of the Lombard king, who is by one writer called Desiderata, and by another

Bertrada. She bore him no children, and on her divorce after something less than a year of matrimony, Charles married Hildegard, a noble Swabian lady, the best beloved of all his wives. Her life, though splendid, was not an easy one. She was only thirteen years old when she married the Frankish hero who was verging on thirty : she accompanied him on his campaigns and pilgrimages : she bore him nine children, and after twelve or thirteen years of wedlock she died on the 30th of April 783, and was buried at Metz in the chapel of St. Arnulf, her husband's revered ancestor. From this marriage sprang all the three sons, Charles, Pippin, Louis, among whom Charlemagne hoped to divide his kingdom, also another son who died in infancy, and five daughters. The eldest of these daughters was that princess Hrotrud who learned Greek of Elissæus, and who so narrowly missed sharing the Byzantine throne.

A few months after the death of Hildegard, Charles married (about October 783) Fastrada, daughter of the Austrasian count Radolf, with whom he shared eleven years of married life, and whose baneful influence on his character and conduct is described to us by Einhard. She bore him two daughters (both of whom eventually became abbesses) but no son, and died on the 10th of August 794, shortly after the great council of Frankfurt.

Not many years after Fastrada's death Charles married his fifth wife, the Alamannian Liutgard, who had previously lived with him as his concubine, and who died on the 4th of June 800, a few months too soon to wear the title of Empress. We are not told of any issue of this marriage, the last legal union which Charles contracted—the magnificent scheme of a marriage alliance with Irene having never been realised. We hear, however, of four additional concubines and several illegitimate children, some of whom rose to high honours in the Church.

The home which the great emperor favoured above all others was that city which his love alone made eminent, though he did not absolutely found it, the city which the Romans called Aquisgranum, which the Germans now call Aachen, and the French Aix-la-Chapelle. Here, on the southern slope of the Lousberg hills, in the pleasant land between Rhine and Meuse, Charles made the dwelling-place of his old age. With all his wide, far-reaching schemes he remained, it would seem, at heart a Ripuarian Frank—Ripuarian not Salian—and we may conjecture that Neustria was to him as little of a homeland as Aquitaine or even Italy. The river Rhine with its great bordering bishoprics, Mainz, Köln, Trier, and its grand Romanesque churches, bore for centuries the character which it had received from the greatest of its sons, the friend alike of Hadrian the Pope and of Alcuin the scholar : and, if not on the actual banks of the Rhine, at least in the near neighbourhood of Rhine-land it was fitting that Charles should die. Doubtless the nature-heated baths which had been known since the time of Severus Alexander, and which are said to have been named from Apollo Granus, were the chief determining causes which led Charles to visit the place, at which indeed his father Pippin had kept Christmas and Easter as long ago as 765. But having visited it, and probably derived benefit from the waters, he evidently became more and more attached to the place. We first hear of Charles keeping his Christmas there in 788 : but after that the name is of frequent recurrence in the Annals till at last Worms and Frankfurt which had before been his favourite abiding-places are almost entirely superseded, and "Imperator celebravit natalem Domini Aquisgrani," becomes the regular formula of the chronicles.

Here, then, at Aachen, Charles built himself a lordly palace and a church, joined together by a colonnade. For both these structures he or his architect, Master Odo, borrowed the plan from Ravenna; the palace being built after the pattern of Theodoric's palace, and the church, which was dedicated to the Virgin Mary, being a copy of that dedicated to San Vitale. Nor was the plan the only thing which was borrowed. Columns and marble tablets were brought from Rome as well as from Ravenna. The mosaics from Theodoric's palace and the equestrian statue in gilded bronze of the great Ostrogoth—a work apparently of more artistic merit than most of the productions of the sixth century, were all carried off from the city on the Ronco to adorn the Belgic palace of the new emperor. Near the palace was a wide-stretching forest surrounded with walls, full of game, resounding with the song of birds and watered by the little stream of the Worm.

Of all these memorials of the great emperor probably nothing now remains but the church. The deer-park has doubtless long since disappeared: of the palace all that can be said is that the Rathhaus is built upon its site: but the *Capella in Palatio* still stands, and is included in the much later building which is known as the Münster. It is about 100 feet high and 50 feet in diameter, surmounted by an octagonal cupola and surrounded by a sixteen-sided cloister. The resemblance to San Vitale at once strikes the visitor who is acquainted with the churches of Ravenna.

It was certainly a triumphant era for the Frankish nation—still *one*, not yet fallen asunder into diverse and hostile nationalities—when the embassies of mighty kings from east and west trod the streets of the little city in Rhine-land which their ruler, sprung, not from a long line of kings but from a family of Austrasian nobles, had made the seat of his empire. Thither came swarthy Saracens from Bagdad, ambassadors from the court—

> Of Haroun, for whose name by blood defiled,
> Genius hath wrought salvation.

Common enmities (for they both were hostile to the Ommayad Caliphs and the eastern emperors), drew together these two men whose names for so long were dear to the story-tellers of east and west, Charlemagne and Haroun-al-Raschid. Haroun sent to Charles in 807 some sort of message or letter confirming the act of the Patriarch of Jerusalem which by the surrender of the keys constituted him guardian of the Holy Places. Some years before he had sent, besides other rich and costly presents, one which especially impressed the minds of the Franks, an enormous elephant named Abu-l-Abbas. Under the guidance of its keeper, Isaac the Jew, the elephant safely reached Aachen, where it abode for eight years. In the year 810 it was taken across the Rhine, apparently that its great strength might be made use of in the expected campaign against Godofrid the Dane; and its sudden death at Lippeham in Westphalia is solemnly recorded by the chroniclers among the memorable events of that melancholy year.

It was in this same year, in the month of October, that the emperor saw with pride two embassies, from east and west, meet at his court. The long delayed overtures for reconciliation from the Emperor Nicephorus were brought by the one, and proposals for a treaty of peace with El Hakem the Cruel, Emir of Cordova, were brought by the other embassy and graciously accepted by Charles.

Nor was our own island unrepresented among the embassies which visited the Frankish Court. With Offa of Mercia, most powerful of English kings before the rise of Ecgbert, the relations were not altogether friendly. A treaty for the marriage of the younger Charles with the daughter of Offa broke down (789), it is said, because of Offa's counter-proposal on behalf of his son for the hand of Charles's daughter Bertha. Some passages in this abortive "double marriage negociation" so annoyed the Frankish king that English merchants were forbidden to land on the shores of Gaul. However, though no marriage was brought to pass, friendly relations between the two kings were restored, perhaps through the mediation of Offa's subject, Alcuin; and in 796 when the great *Hring* of the Avars had been despoiled by Eric of Friuli, an Avar sword was graciously sent by Charles as a present to the King of Mercia.

It was not at Aachen but at Nimeguen on the Rhine that another English king, driven from his realm by revolution, Eardulf of Northumberland, visited Charles's court in 808 and besought his aid to restore him to his throne. Charles seems to have embraced his cause and sent him on to Rome with a letter of recommendation to Pope Leo whose help was needed, as the Archbishop of York had taken an active part in Eardulf's deposition. With the help of emperor and pope, Eardulf was restored (809) to a throne which he seems to have justly forfeited by various acts of tyranny; but the reign of the restored king was of short duration.

It may be permitted to conjecture that the happiest period of the life of Charles consisted of the fifteen years which he spent mainly at Aachen between 795 and 810. The Saxon and Avar wars were drawing to a close, his labours for the reform of the Church and for the spread of learning were bearing manifest fruit: the haughty and difficult-tempered Fastrada was dead, and his children, whom he loved with fondness not often found in palaces, were growing up around him. The few words in which Einhard sketches his family life give one an impression of joyous magnificence not unlike that which the poets have feigned concerning the purely imaginary court of King Arthur :—

"He determined so to bring up his children that all, both sons and daughters, should be well grounded in liberal studies, to which he himself also gave earnest attention. Moreover, he caused his sons as soon as they were of the proper age to learn to ride after the manner of the Franks, to be trained to war and the chase: but his daughters he ordered to learn the spinning of wool, to give heed to the spindle and distaff, that they might not grow slothful through ease, but be trained to all kinds of honest industry. . . .

"So great was the attention which he paid to the education of his sons and daughters that when he was at home he would never sup without them; when he journeyed they must accompany him, the sons riding by his side and the daughters following a little behind, while a band of servants appointed for this purpose brought up the rear. As for these daughters, though they were of great beauty and were dearly loved by him, strange to say he never gave one of them in marriage either to a man of his own nation or to a foreigner, but he kept them all with him in his own house till his death, saying that he could not dispense with their company. On this account, prosperous as he was in other ways, he experienced the unkindness of adverse fortune, as to which, however, he so skilfully dissembled that no one would suppose that any suspicion of a stain on their fair fame had ever reached his ears."

This last sentence of Charles's usually enthusiastic biographer hints at court scandals which could not be always concealed, and the results of some of which appear in the Carolingian pedigrees. But the previous statement concerning his unwillingness to have his merry family circle broken in upon by the unwelcome claims of a son-in-law, may possibly help to explain what has perplexed us in the rupture of the matrimonial treaty with Byzantium or even with the King of Mercia. Instead of seeking for deep state-reasons of policy for these failures, we ought, perhaps, simply to see in them the pardonable weakness of a father who, when the crisis came, gave more heed to the voice of family affection than to the maxims of state-craft.

A notice of Charles's home life would be incomplete without some allusion to the circle of friends by whom he was surrounded, and whom he seems to have inspired with a genuine love for himself as a man, apart from their loyalty to him as sovereign.

The great ecclesiastics who, under the name of Arch-chaplains, held a place similar to that of a modern prime minister, Fulrad, Abbot of St. Denis, who had been chaplain to his father and who died in 784; his successor Angilram, Bishop of Metz, who died while accompanying Charles on his Avar campaign in 791; Hildibald, Archbishop of Cologne, who stood by the emperor's death-bed: all these men, though highly trusted and able servants, have not left many evidences by which we can judge of their individual characters. Much more interesting is Charles's relation to the men of letters whom he delighted to gather around him. Chief among these were Alcuin, Peter of Pisa, Paul the Lombard, and Einhard.

Of Alcuin, who might truly be called Charles's literary prime minister, no more need be said, save that he died at Tours in 804, full of years and in unclouded friendship with the emperor.

It was apparently about the year 780 that Peter of Pisa, a deacon who had once taught in the Lombard capital, Pavia, and had there held a celebrated disputation with a Jew named Lullus, came to Charles's court. He was then an old man. Grammar was his main subject, and Charles regularly attended his lectures. The date of his death is uncertain, but it was before the year 799.

Paul the Lombard, generally known as Paulus Diaconus, probably made Charles's acquaintance during his second visit to Italy (780-781). At any rate, somewhere about the year 782 he followed Charles across the

Alps, and was for some two or three years in pretty close
attendance at the Frankish court. The main object of
his journey was to obtain pardon and the restitution of
confiscated property for his brother Arichis who, as has
been already stated, seems to have been involved in the
rebellion of Duke Hrodgaud, and was carried captive
into Frankland, leaving his wife and children destitute.
There can be little doubt that the pardon of Arichis
was granted to the intercession of his brother, for
whom Charles seems to have conceived an especial
affection. An amusing but fearfully perplexing series
of poems exists, in which enigmas, compliments, and
good-natured banter are exchanged between the king,
Paulus Diaconus, and Petrus Pisanus. At dawn of
day a trim young courtier with a hopeful little beard
brings to Peter the grammarian a riddle which the king
has thought of in the night and desires him to guess it.
In despair Peter turns to Paul begging for his aid. In
a hexameter poem of forty-seven lines (all the correspondence is in verse) Paul gives his version of the
answer, which, if correct, certainly proves the riddle to
have been a very foolish one. At another time the king
poetically asks Paul which of three penalties he would
prefer—to be crushed under an immense weight of iron,
to be doomed to lie in a gloomy dungeon-cave, or to be sent
to convert and baptize Sigfrid who "wields the impious
sceptre of pestilential Denmark." Paul replies in a
strain of enthusiastic devotion that he will do anything
which the king desires him to do, but that as he knows
no Danish he will seem like a brute beast when he
stands in the presence of the barbarian king. Yet
would he have no fear for his own safety if he under-

took the journey: for if Sigfrid knew that he was one of Charles's subjects, so great is his dread of the Frankish king that he would not dare to touch him with his little finger. And so on through many hexameter and pentameter verses. A harsh critic might describe the whole correspondence as "gracious fooling," but in view of the hard and toilsome life of the slayer and converter of so many Saxons, it is a consolation to find that he had leisure and spare brain-power even for occasional nonsense.

Paulus Diaconus, after a few years' sojourn at the Frankish court, returned to Italy to the shelter of his beloved convent of Monte Cassino, where he died, probably in one of the closing years of the eighth century. We are indebted to him, not only for his well-known *Historia Langobardorum*—almost the only record of the history of Italy from 568 to 744—but also for a book on the *Gesta Episcoporum Mettensium* which gives us valuable information as to the lives of the early Arnulfings.

The last of Charles's literary courtiers who can be noticed here is Einhard or (as his name is commonly but less correctly written) Eginhard. This man, who was born near the time of Charles's accession to the kingdom, and who survived him about thirty years, was the son of Einhard and Engilfrita, persons of good birth and station who dwelt in Franconia near the Odenwald. He was educated in the monastery of Fulda, and came as a young man to the Frankish court, where his nimbleness of mind, his learning and his skill in the administration of affairs so recommended him to Charles that for the remaining twenty years or more of

his reign the little Franconian—he was a man of conspicuously short stature—was the great king's inseparable
companion. His skill in all manner of metal work
earned for him in that name-giving circle of friends the
name of Bezaleel, by which he is pleasantly alluded
to in one of Alcuin's letters. He was employed to
superintend some of Charles's great architectural works :
notably the palace and basilica at Aachen, the palace at
Ingelheim and the great bridge over the Rhine at
Mainz. A twelfth-century chronicler connected his
name unpleasantly with that of one of the daughters
of Charles : but for this scandal there does not seem
to be the slightest foundation. None of Charles's
daughters was named Emma, the name attributed
to the alleged mistress, afterwards wife, of Einhard.
His real wife appears to have been Emma, sister of
Bernhard, Bishop of Worms. About the year 826 he
and his wife parted by mutual consent and "gave
themselves to religion." He was ordained priest and
retired to the monastery of Seligenstadt on the Main
where he died about the year 840.

Einhard had a share (how large is a subject of
constant discussion), in the composition of the official
Annals which are our most trustworthy authority for
the history of his master's reign. But we are far more
indebted to him for his short tract *De Vitâ Caroli Magni*
from which several extracts have already been made. In
this life there is an evident ambition on the part of the
writer, who calls himself "a barbarian little skilled in
Roman speech" to follow the example of the great classical authors. His imitation, especially, of the Life of
Augustus by Suetonius, is almost servile, and provokes

much laughter on the part of modern scholars; but however he may be derided, the fact remains that almost all our real, vivifying knowledge of Charles the Great is derived from Einhard, and that the *Vita Caroli* is one of the most precious literary bequests of the early Middle Ages.

Here are some features of the picture of his master by Einhard which have not been copied in the preceding pages :—

"This king, whose prudence and magnanimity surpassed that of all contemporary princes, never shunned on account of toil, nor declined on account of danger, any enterprise which had to be begun or carried through to its end; but having learned to bear every burden as it came, according to its true weight, he would neither yield under adversity, nor in prosperity trust the flattering smiles of fortune."

"He loved foreigners and took the greatest pains to entertain them, so that their number often seemed a real burden, not only to the palace but even to the realm. But he, on account of his greatness of soul, refused to worry himself over this burden, thinking that even great inconveniences were amply compensated by the praise of his liberality and the reward of his renown."

"His gait was firm, all the habit of his body manly : his voice clear, but scarce corresponding to his stature : his health good, except that during the last four years of his life he was often attacked by fever, and at the last he limped with one foot. Moreover he guided himself much more by his own fancy than by the counsel of his physicians, whom he almost hated because they tried to

persuade him to give up roast meats, to which he was
accustomed, and to take to boiled. He kept up
diligently his exercises of riding and hunting, wherein
he followed the usage of his nation, for scarcely any
other race equals the Franks herein. He delighted, too,
in the steam of nature-heated baths, being a frequent
and skilful swimmer, so that hardly any one excelled
him in this exercise. This was his reason for building
his palace at Aquisgranum where he spent the latter
years of his life up to his death. And not only did he
invite his sons to the bath, but also his friends and the
nobles, sometimes even a crowd of henchmen and body-
guards, so that at times as many as a hundred men or
more would be bathing there together."

" He was temperate in food and drink, especially the
latter, since he held drunkenness in any man, but most
of all in himself and his friends, in the highest
abhorrence. He was not so well able to abstain from
food, and used often to complain that the fasts [of the
Church] were hurtful to his body. He very seldom
gave banquets, and those only on the chief festivals, but
then he invited a very large number of guests. His
daily supper was served with four courses only, except
the roast, which the huntsmen used to bring in on spits,
and which he partook of more willingly than of any other
food. During supper he listened either to music or to
the reading of some book, generally histories and accounts
of the things done by the ancients. He delighted also in
the writings of St. Augustine, especially that one which
is entitled *De Civitate Dei*. He was so chary of drinking
wine or liquor of any kind, that he seldom drank more
than three times at supper. In summer, after his mid-

day meal, he would take some fruit and would drink once, and then laying aside his raiment and his shoes, just as he was wont to do at night, he would rest for two or three hours. At night his sleep used to be interrupted, not only by awaking but by rising from his bed four or five times in one night. When he was having his shoes or his clothes put on he used not only to admit his friends, but even if the Count of the Palace informed him of some law-suit which could not be settled without his order, he would direct the litigants to be at once introduced into his presence, and would hear the cause and pronounce sentence exactly as if he were sitting on the judgment seat. And not only so, but he would also at the same time tell each official or servant of the palace what duty he had to perform that day."

" He was full even to overflowing in his eloquence, and could express all his ideas with very great clearness. And not being satisfied with his native language alone, he also gave much attention to the learning of foreign tongues, among which was Latin, which he learned so perfectly that he was accustomed to pray indifferently in that language or in his own. Greek, however, he learned to understand better than to pronounce. He was in truth so eloquent that he seemed like a professional rhetorician. In learning grammar he attended the lectures of Peter of Pisa, an old man and a deacon: in other studies he had for his teacher another deacon, Albinus, surnamed Alcuin, from Britain, a man of Saxon race and extremely learned in all subjects, with whom he gave a great deal of time and toil to the study of rhetoric and dialectic, and pre-eminently to that of astronomy. He learned the art of computation, and with wise earnestness most carefully investigated the courses of the stars. He tried also to write, and for this purpose used to carry about with him tablets and manuscripts [to copy] which were placed under the pillows of his bed in order that he might at odd times accustom his fingers to the shaping of the letters : but the attempt was made too late in life and was not successful."

"He was a devout and zealous upholder of the Christian religion, with which he had been imbued from infancy. He regularly attended the church which he had built at Aquisgranum morning and evening, and also in the hours of the night and at the time of sacrifice, as far as his health permitted; and he took great pains that all the rites celebrated therein should be performed with the greatest decorum, constantly admonishing the ministers of the church that they should not allow anything dirty or unbecoming to be brought thither or to remain within it. He provided so large a supply of holy vessels of gold and silver and of priestly vestments, that in celebrating the sacrifices there was no necessity even for the doorkeepers, who were of the lowest grade of ecclesiastics, to minister in their private dress. He took great pains to reform the style of reading and singing, in both of which he was highly accomplished, though he did not himself read in public nor sing, save in a low voice and with the rest of the congregation."

"He was very earnest in the maintenance of the poor and in almsgiving, so that not only in his own country and kingdom did he thus labour, but also beyond sea. To Syria, to Egypt, to Africa, to Jerusalem, to Carthage, wherever he heard that there were Christians living in poverty, he was wont to send money as a proof of his sympathy, and for this reason especially did he seek the friendship of transmarine kings, in order that some refreshment and relief might come to the Christians under their rule. But before all other sacred and venerable places he reverenced the church of St. Peter at Rome, and in its treasure chamber great store of wealth, in gold, silver, and precious stones was piled up by him. Many gifts, past counting, were sent by him to the popes, and through the whole of his reign no object was dearer to his heart than that the city of Rome by his care and toil should enjoy its old pre-eminence, and that the church of St. Peter should not only by his aid be safely guarded, but also by his resources should be adorned and enriched beyond all other churches. Yet though he esteemed that city so highly, in all the forty-seven years of his reign he went but four times thither to pay his vows and offer up his supplications."

Amid such interests and such friendships the later years of Charles's life glided away, comparatively little disturbed by the clash of arms, since his two elder sons Charles and Pippin, brave and capable men both of them, now relieved him of most of the drudgery of war. It is hinted that there were some occasions of variance between the two brothers, but it is not certain that Pippin the Hunchback is not the person here alluded to as at enmity with the younger Charles; and the difference, whatever it may have been, is said to have been removed by the mediation of St. Goar, whose cell on the banks of the Rhine was visited by the two princes.

In 806, at the Villa Theodonis, Charles, in the presence of a great assembly of his nobles, made a formal division of his dominions between his three sons. Pippin was to have Italy, or as it was called, Langobardia, with Bavaria and Germany south of the Danube, also the subject realms of the Avars and southern Sclaves. Louis was to have Aquitaine, Provence, and the greater part of Burgundy. All the rest, that is Neustria, Austrasia, the remainder of Burgundy, and Germany north of the Danube was to go to Charles, who was probably to have some sort of pre-eminence over his brothers, though nothing was expressly said as to the imperial title. The division was so ordered that each brother had access to the dominions of the other two, and both Charles and Louis were earnestly enjoined to go to the help of Pippin—then apparently the most exposed to hostile attack—if he should require their help in Italy. Elaborate arrangements were also made as to the succession, in case of the death of any of the brothers.

Unhappily all these dispositions proved futile. The year 810, in which Godofrid of Denmark died, and also Haroun's elephant Abu-l-Abbas, was in other ways a sore year for Charles. On 6th June his eldest daughter Hrotrud, once the affianced bride of the Eastern Cæsar, died, unmarried but leaving an illegitimate son, Louis, who afterwards became Abbot of St. Denis. Ere Charles had time to recover from this blow came the tidings that Pippin, the young King of Italy, had died on 8th July, possibly (but this is only a conjecture) of some malady contracted during his campaign of many months among the lagunes of Venice.

So, though Pippin left a son, the lad Bernhard, who, if things went well with him, might hope to inherit his father's kingdom, already a breach was made in Charles's arrangements for the succession to his dominions.   But a yet heavier blow fell upon him next year (4th December 811), when his eldest son Charles, that one of all his children who most resembled him in aptitude for war and government, in strength of body and manly beauty, was torn from him by death.   Now, of all his sons, there was only left that pathetically devout and incapable figure who is known to posterity as Louis the Pious or Louis the Debonnair, but whose piety and whose good nature were alike to prove disastrous when he should be called upon to guide with his nerveless hands the fiery steeds which had drawn his father's car of empire.

However, there was no other heir available.   In September 813 a *generalis conventus* was held at Aachen, at which, after taking the advice of his nobles, Charles placed the imperial crown on the head of Louis, and ordered him to be called Imperator and Augustus, thereby designating him as his successor, but not, as it should seem, admitting him to a present participation in his power.   With that keen insight into character which Charles undoubtedly possessed, he must have perceived the weakness of his son's disposition, and fears for the future of the empire which he had built up with so much toil and difficulty probably saddened his last days.

The great emperor had now entered on the eighth decade of his life.   His health was apparently failing, and there were also signs and portents betokening the approaching end, which, with proper regard to classical precedent, are duly recorded by Einhard. For the last three years of his life there was an unusually large number of eclipses of the sun and moon. A big spot on the sun was observed for seven days. The colonnade between the church and palace at Aachen, constructed with great labour, fell in sudden ruin on Ascension-day. The great bridge over the Rhine at Mainz, which had been ten years in building, and for which Einhard himself had acted as clerk of the works, was burnt to the water's edge in three hours. Then, in his last expedition against Danish Godofrid (but that was as far back as 810), a fiery torch had been seen to fall from heaven, in a clear sky, on the sinister side, and Charles's horse at the same moment falling heavily had thrown his master to the ground with such violence that the clasp of his cloak was broken, his sword-belt burst, and the spear which he held in his hand was hurled forwards twenty feet or more. Moreover there were crackings of the palace-ceilings; the golden apple which was on the roof of the church was struck by lightning and thrown on to the roof of the archbishop's palace hard by. In the inscription which ran round the interior of the dome, and which contained the words KAROLVS PRINCEPS, the letters of the second word, only a few months before Charles's death, faded and became invisible. All these signs convinced thoughtful persons that an old man of more than seventy, who had led a hard and strenuous life, and who was bowed by many recent sorrows, had not long to live.

In the year 811, the emperor, feeling that the end was not far off, had given elaborate orders as to the disposal of his personal property, consisting of gold, silver, and precious stones. The details, though curious, need not be quoted here. It is sufficient to say that only one-twelfth of the whole was to be divided among his children and grand-children. About two-thirds were to be divided among the ecclesiastics of twenty-one chief cities in his dominions. The remainder was for his servants and the poor. It is interesting to observe that the division of the property was to be completed "after his death or voluntary renunciation of the things of this world." There was therefore a possibility that the first Emperor Charles might have anticipated the fifth in retiring from a palace into a convent. Also we note with interest a square silver table containing a plan of the city of Constantinople, which was to be sent as a gift to St. Peter's at Rome; a round one containing a similar plan of Rome, which was to be sent to the Archbishop of Ravenna; and a third, "far surpassing the others in weight of metal and beauty of workman-ship, which consisted of three spheres linked together, and which embraced a plan of the whole world with delicate and minute delineation," and which was to be sold for the benefit of the residuary legatees and the poor.

At last the time came for all these dispositions to take effect. After the great assembly in which the imperial diadem was placed on the head of Louis of Aquitaine (Sept. 813), Charles, though in feeble health, went on one of his usual hunting expeditions in the neighbourhood of Aachen. The autumn was thus passed, and at the begin-ning of November he returned to the palace to winter there. In January (814) he was attacked by a severe fever and took to his bed. According to his usual custom he thought to subdue the fever by fasting, but pleurisy was added to the fever, and in his reduced state he had no power to grapple with the disease. After partaking of the Communion he departed this life at nine in the morning of the 28th of January 814. He was then in the seventy-second year of his age, and the forty-seventh of his reign. On the day of his death he was buried in his own church of St. Mary, amidst the lamentations of his people. On a gilded arch above his tomb was inscribed this epitaph. "Under this tomb-stone is laid the body of Charles, the great and orthodox Emperor, who gloriously enlarged the kingdom of the Franks and reigned prosperously for 47 years (*sic*). He died, a septuagenarian, in the year of our Lord 814, in the 7th Indiction on the 5th day before the Kalends of February."

Before many years had passed, the adjective *Magnus* was universally affixed by popular usage to the name *Carolus:* and 351 years after his death he received the honour of canonisation from the Roman Church.

CHAPTER XIII

No ruler for many centuries so powerfully impressed the imagination of western Europe as the first Frankish Emperor of Rome. The vast cycle of romantic epic poetry which gathered round the name of Charlemagne, the stories of his wars with the Infidels, his expeditions to Constantinople and Jerusalem, his Twelve Peers of France, the friendship of Roland and Oliver and the treachery of Ganelon—all this is of matchless interest in the history of the development of mediæval literature, but of course adds nothing to our knowledge of the real Charles of history, since these romances were confessedly the work of wandering minstrels and took no definite shape till at least three centuries after the death of Charlemagne.

In this concluding chapter I propose very briefly to enumerate some of the chief traces of the great emperor's forming hand on the western church, on Literature, on Laws, and on the State-system of Europe.

I. Theologically, Charles's chief performances were the condemnation of the Adoptianist heresy of Felix of Urgel by the Council of Frankfurt (794): the condemnation of the adoration of images by the same Council; and the addition to the Nicene Creed of the celebrated words "Filioque," which asserted that the Holy Spirit "proceedeth from the Father *and the Son.*" In these two last performances Charles acted more or less in opposition to the advice and judgment of the pope, and the addition to the Creed was one of the causes which led to the schism between the eastern and western churches, and which have hitherto frustrated all schemes for their reunion.

In the government of the church Charles all through his reign took the keenest interest, and a large—as most modern readers would think a disproportionate—part of his Capitularies is dedicated to this subject. Speaking generally, it may be said that he strove, as his father before him had striven, to subdue the anarchy that had disgraced the churches of Gaul under the Merovingian kings. He insisted on the monks and the canonical priests living according to the rules which they professed: he discouraged the manufacture of new saints, the erection of new oratories, the worship of new archangels other than the well-known three, Gabriel, Michael, and Raphael. He earnestly exhorted the bishops to work in harmony with the counts for the maintenance of the public peace. While not slow to condemn the faults of the episcopacy he supported their authority against mutinous priests: and pre-eminently, by the example which he set to Gaul in the powerful and well-compacted hierarchy which he established in Germany, he strengthened the aristocratic constitution of the church under the rule of its bishops. At the same time there can be no doubt that by his close relations with the Roman Pontiff and by the temporal sovereignty which he bestowed upon him, he contributed, consciously or unconsciously, to the ultimate transformation of the western church into an absolute monarchy under the headship of the pope. That Charles, with all his zeal for the welfare of the church, was not blind to the faults of the churchmen of his day is shown by the remarkable series of questions—possibly drawn up from his dictation by Einhard—which are contained in a Capitulary of 811 written three years before his death :

"We wish to ask the ecclesiastics themselves, and those who have not only to learn but to teach out of the Holy Scriptures, who are they to whom the Apostle says, 'Be ye imitators of me': or who that is about whom the same Apostle says, 'No man that warreth entangleth himself with the business of this world': in other words, how the Apostle is to be imitated, or how he (the ecclesiastic) wars for God ?"

"Further, we must beg of them that they will truly show us what is this 'renouncing of the world' which is spoken of by them: or how we can distinguish those who renounce the world from those who still follow it, whether it consists in anything more than this, that they do not bear arms and are not publicly married ?"

"We must also enquire if that man has relinquished the world who is daily labouring to increase his possessions in every manner and by every artifice, by sweet persuasions about the blessedness of heaven and by terrible threats about the punishments of hell; who uses the name of God or of some saint to despoil simpler and less learned folk, whether rich or poor, of their property, to deprive the lawful heirs of their inheritance and thus to drive many through sheer destitution to a life of robbery and crime which they would otherwise never have embraced ?"

Several more questions of an equally searching character are contained in this remarkable Capitulary.

II. If doubts may arise in some minds how far Charles's ecclesiastical policy was of permanent benefit to the human race, no such doubts can be felt as to his patronage of literature and science. Herein he takes a foremost place among the benefactors of humanity, as a man who, himself imperfectly educated, knew how to value education in others; as one who, amid the manifold harassing cares of government and of war, could find leisure for that friendly intercourse with learned men which far more than his generous material gifts cheered them on in their arduous and difficult work ; and as the ruler to whom more perhaps than to any other single individual we owe the fact that the precious literary inheritance of Greece and Rome has not been altogether lost to the human race. Every student of the history of the texts of the classical authors knows how many of our best MSS. date from the ninth century, the result unquestionably of the impulse given by Charles and his learned courtiers to classical studies. It is noticeable also that this reign constitutes an important era in Paleography, the clear and beautiful "minuscule" of the Irish scribes being generally substituted for the sprawling and uncouth characters which had gone by the name of Langobardic. In one of his Capitularies Charles calls the attention of his clergy to the necessity for careful editing of the Prayer-books; otherwise those who desire to pray rightly will pray amiss. He enjoins them not to suffer boys to corrupt the sacred text either in writing or reading. If they require a new gospel, missal, or psalter, let it be copied with the utmost care by men of full age. In another Capitulary, he expresses his displeasure that some priests, who were poor when they were ordained, have grown rich out of the church's treasures, acquiring for themselves lands and slaves, but not purchasing books or sacred vessels for the church's use.

Something has already been said as to the Academy in Charles's palace, which was apparently founded on the basis of a court-school established in his father's lifetime, but became a much more important institution in his own. Probably it was then transformed from a school for children into an Academy for learned men, in the sense in which the word has been used at Athens, Florence, and Paris. Alcuin, after his departure from court, founded a school at Tours, which acquired great fame; and we hear of schools also at Utrecht, Fulda, Würzburg, and elsewhere. Doubtless, most of these schools were primarily theological seminaries, but, as we have seen in the case of Alcuin, a good deal of classical literature and mathematical science was, at any rate in some schools, taught alongside of the correct rendering of the church service.

The Monk of St. Gall (who wrote, as we have seen, two generations after Charlemagne, and whose stories we therefore accept with some reserve) gives us an interesting and amusing picture of one of the schools under Charles's patronage. After giving a legendary and inaccurate account of the arrival of two Irish

scholars in Gaul, named Alcuin and Clement, he goes on
to say that Charles persuaded Clement to settle in Gaul,
and sent him a number of boys, sons of nobles, of
middle-class men and of peasants, to be taught by him,
while they were lodged and boarded at the king's
charges. After a long time he returned to Gaul, and
ordered these lads to be brought into his presence, and
to bring before him letters and poems of their own
composition. The boys sprung from the middle and
lower classes offered compositions which were "beyond
all expectation sweetened with the seasoning of wisdom,"
but the productions of the young nobility were "tepid,
and absolutely idiotic." Hereupon the king, as it were,
anticipating the Last Judgment, set the industrious lads
on his right hand and the idlers on his left. He
addressed the former with words of encouragement, "I
thank you, my sons, for the zeal with which you have
attended to my commands. Only go on as you have
begun, and I will give you splendid bishoprics and
abbacies, and you shall be ever honourable in my eyes."
But to those on his left hand he turned with angry eyes
and frowning brow, and addressed them in a voice of
thunder, "You young nobles, you dainty and beautiful
youths, who have presumed upon your birth and your
possessions to despise mine orders, and have taken no
care for my renown; you have neglected the study of
literature, while you have given yourselves over to
luxury and idleness, or to games and foolish athletics."
Then, raising his august head and unconquered right
hand towards heaven, he swore a solemn oath, "By the
King of Heaven, I care nothing for your noble birth
and your handsome faces, let others prize them as they

may.   Know this for certain, that unless ye give earnest
heed to your studies, and recover the ground lost by
your negligence, ye shall never receive any favour at the
hand of King Charles."

There was one branch of learning in which Charles
was evidently not enough helped by his friends of the
classical revival, and in which one cannot help wishing
that his judgment had prevailed over theirs.   Einhard
tells us that he reduced to writing and committed to
memory "those most ancient songs of the barbarians in
which the actions of the kings of old and their wars
were chanted."   Would that these precious relics of the
dim Teutonic fore-world had been thought worthy of
preservation by Alcuin and his disciples !

He also began to compose a grammar of his native
speech ; he gave names to the winds blowing from
twelve different quarters, whereas previously men had
named but four ; and he gave Teutonic instead of Latin
names to the twelve months of the year.   They were—
for January, *Wintarmanoth ;* February, *Hornung ;* March,
Lentzinmanoth ; April, *Ostarmanoth ;* May, *Winnemanoth ;*
June, *Brachmanoth ;* July, *Hewimanoth ;* August, *Aran-
manoth ;* September, *Witumanoth ;* October, *Windumema-
noth ;* November, *Herbistmanoth ;* December, *Heilagmanoth.*

III. It is of course impossible to deal with more than
one or two of the most important products of Charles's
legislative and administrative activity.

1. In the first place, we have to remark that Charles
was not in any sense like Justinian or Napoleon, a
codifier of laws.   On the contrary, the title chosen by
him after his capture of Pavia, "Rex Langobardorum,"

indicates the general character of his policy, which was
to leave the Lombards under Lombard law, the Romans
under Roman law; even the Saxons, if they would only
accept Christianity, to some extent under Saxon institutions.   To turn all the various nationalities over which
he ruled into Ripuarian Franks was by no means the
object of the conqueror; on the contrary, so long as
they loyally obeyed the great central government they
might keep their own laws, customs, and language
unaltered.   As this principle applied not only to tribes
and races of men, but also to individuals, we find ourselves in presence of that most peculiar phenomenon of
the early Middle Ages which is known as the system of
"personal law."   In our modern society, if the citizen
of one country goes to reside in the territory of another
civilised and well-ordered country, he is bound to con-
form to the laws of that country.   Where this rule does
not prevail (as in the case of the rights secured by the
"capitulations" to Europeans dwelling in Turkey or
Morocco) it is a distinct sign that we are in the presence
of a barbarous law to which the more civilised nations
will not submit.   But quite different from this was the
conception of law in the ninth century under Charles
the Great and his successors.   Then, every man, according to his nationality, or even his profession,—according
as he was Frank or Lombard, Alaman or Bavarian, Goth
or Roman, layman or ecclesiastic,—carried, so to speak,
his own legal atmosphere about with him, and might
always claim to be judged *secundum legem patriae suae*.
Thus, according to an often-quoted passage, "so great
was the diversity of laws that you would often meet
with it, not only in countries or cities, but even in

single houses. For it would often happen that five men would be sitting or walking together, not one of whom would have the same law with any other."

But though Charles made no attempt, and apparently had no desire, to reduce all the laws of his subjects to one common denominator, he had schemes for improving, and even to some extent harmonising, the several national codes which he found in existence. But these schemes were only imperfectly realised. As Einhard says, "After his assumption of the imperial title, as he perceived that many things were lacking in the laws of his people (for the Franks have two systems of law, in many places very diverse from one another), he thought to add those things which were wanting, to reconcile discrepancies, and to correct what was bad and ill expressed. But of all this naught was accomplished by him, save that he added a few chapters, and those imperfect ones, to the laws [of the Salians, Ripuarians, and Bavarians]. All the legal customs, however, that were not already written, of the various nations under his dominion, he caused to be taken down and committed to writing."

While Charles's new legislation was in general of an enlightened and civilised character, a modern reader is surprised and pained by the prominence which he gives, or allows, to those barbarous and superstitious modes of determining doubtful causes—wager of battle, ordeal by the cross, and ordeal by the hot ploughshares. As to the first of these especially, the language of the Capitularies seems to show a retrogression from the wise distrust of that manner of arriving at truth expressed half a century earlier by the Lombard king, Liutprand.

2. A question which we cannot help asking, though it hardly admits of an answer, is, "What was Charles's relation to that feudal system which, so soon after his death, prevailed throughout his empire, and which so quickly destroyed its unity?" The growth of that system was so gradual, and it was due to such various causes, that no one man can be regarded as its author, hardly even to any great extent as its modifier. It was not known to early Merovingian times; its origin appears to be nearly contemporaneous with that of the power of the Arnulfing mayors of the palace; it must certainly have been spreading more widely and striking deeper roots all through the reign of Charlemagne, and yet we can hardly attribute either to him or to his ancestors any distinct share in its establishment. It was, so to speak, "in the air," even as democracy, trades' unions, socialism, and similar ideas are in the air of the nineteenth century. Feudalism apparently had to be, and it "sprang and grew up, one knoweth not how."

One of the clearest allusions to the growing feudalism of society is contained in a Capitulary of Charles issued the year before his death, in which it is ordained that no man shall be allowed to renounce his dependence on a feudal superior after he has received any benefit from him, except in one of four cases—if the lord have sought to slay his vassal, or have struck him with a stick, or have endeavoured to dishonour his wife or daughter, or to take away his inheritance. In an expanded version of the same decree a fifth cause of renunciation is admitted—if the lord have failed to give to the vassal that protection which he promised when the vassal put his hands in the lord's, and "commended" himself to his guardianship.   Other allusions to the same system are to be found in the numerous Capitularies in which Charles urges the repeated complaint that the vassals of the Crown are either endeavouring to turn their *beneficia* into *allodia*, or, if possessing property of both kinds,—a *beneficium* under the Crown and an *allodium* by purchase or inheritance from their fathers,—are starving and despoiling the royal *beneficium* for the benefit of their own *allodium.*

3. An institution which was intended to check these and similar irregularities, and generally to uphold the imperial authority and the rights of the humbler classes against the encroachments of the territorial aristocracy, was the peculiarly Carolingian institution of *missi dominici*, or (as we may translate the words) "imperial commissioners."   These men may be likened to the emperor's staff-officers, bearing his orders to distant regions, and everywhere, as his representatives, carrying on his ceaseless campaign against oppression and anarchy.   The pivot of provincial government was still, as it had been in Merovingian times, the Frankish *comes* or count, who had his headquarters generally in one of the old Roman cities, and governed from thence a district which was of varying extent, but which may be fairly taken as equivalent to an English county. Under him were the *centenarii*, who, originally rulers of that little tract of country known as the Hundred, now had a somewhat wider scope, and acted probably as *vicarii* or representatives of the count throughout the district subject to his jurisdiction.   These governors, especially the count, were doubtless generally men of

wealth and great local influence. They had not yet succeeded in making their offices hereditary and transmitting the countship, as a title of nobility is now transmitted, from father to son. The strong hand of the central government prevented this change from taking place in Charles's day, but it, too, like so much else that had a feudal tendency, was "in the air"; and it may have been partly in order to guard against this tendency and to keep his counts merely life-governors that Charles devised his institution of *missi*.

But a nobler and more beneficial object aimed at was to ensure that justice should be "truly and indifferently administered" to both rich and poor, to the strong and to the defenceless. It is interesting in this connection to observe what was the so-called "eight-fold ban" proclaimed by the Frankish legislator. Any one who (1) dishonoured Holy Church; (2) or acted unjustly against widows; (3) or against orphans; (4) or against poor men who were unable to defend themselves; (5) or carried off a free-born woman against the will of her parents; (6) or set on fire another man's house or stable; (7) or who committed *harizhut*—that is to say, who broke open by violence another man's house, door, or enclosure; (8) or who when summoned did not go forth against the enemy, came under the king's *ban*, and was liable to pay for each offence sixty solidi (£36). Here we see that three of the specified offences were precisely those which a powerful local count or *centenarius* would be tempted to commit against the humbler suitors in his court, and which it would be the business of a *missus dominicus* to discover and report to his lord.

The *missi* had, however, a wide range of duties beyond

the mere control and correction of unjust judges. It was theirs to enforce the rights of the royal treasury, to administer the oath of allegiance to the inhabitants of a district, to enquire into any cases of wrongful appropriation of church property, to hunt down robbers, to report upon the morals of bishops, to see that monks lived according to the rule of their order. Sometimes they had to command armies (the brave Gerold of Bavaria was such a *missus*) and to hold *placita* in the name of the king. Of course the choice of a person to act as *missus* would largely depend on the nature of the duties that he had to perform : a soldier for the command of armies or an ecclesiastic for the inspection of monasteries. As Charles, in his embassies to foreign courts, was fond of combining the two vocations, and sending a stout layman and a subtle ecclesiastic together to represent him at Cordova or Constantinople, so he may often have duplicated these internal embassies, these roving commissions, to enquire into the abuses of authority in his own dominions.

We have, in one of Charles's later Capitularies, an admirable exhortation which, though put forth in the name of the *missi*, surely came from the emperor's own robust intellect : — "Take care," the *missi* say to the count whose district they are about to visit, "that neither you nor any of your officers are so evil disposed as to say 'Hush ! hush ! say nothing about that matter till those *missi* have passed by, and afterwards we will settle it quietly among ourselves.' Do not so deny or even postpone the administration of justice ; but rather give diligence that justice may be done in the case before we arrive."

The institution of *missi dominici* served its purpose for a time, but proved to be only a temporary expedient. There was an increasing difficulty in finding suitable men for this delicate charge, which required in those who had to execute it both strength and sympathy, an independent position, and willingness to listen to the cry of the humble. Even already in the lifetime of Charles there was a visible danger that the *missus* might become another oppressor as burdensome to the common people as any of the counts whom he was appointed to superintend. And after all, the *missus* could only transmit to the distant regions of the empire as much power as he received from its centre. Under the feeble Louis the Pious, his wrangling sons and his inept grandsons, the institution grew ever weaker and weaker. Admirable instructions for the guidance of the *missi* were drawn up at headquarters, but there was no power to enforce them. With the collapse of the Carolingian dynasty towards the close of the ninth century the *missi dominici* disappear from view.

4. Another institution was perhaps due to Charles's own personal initiative; at any rate it was introduced at the outset of his reign, and soon spread widely through his dominions. It was that of the *scabini*, whose functions recall to us sometimes those of our justices of the peace, sometimes those of our grand-jurors, and sometimes those of our ordinary jurors. Chosen for life, out of the free, but not probably out of the powerful classes, men of respectable character and unstained by crime, they had, besides other functions, pre-eminently that of acting as assessors to the *comes* or to the *centenarius* in his court of

justice. Seven was the regular number that should be present at a trial, though sometimes fewer were allowed to decide. As in all the earlier stages of the development of the jury system, they were at least as much witnesses as judges—their own knowledge or common report forming the chief ground of their decision. It is not clear whether their verdict was necessarily unanimous, but it seems certain that the decision was considered to be theirs, and not that of the presiding functionary, whether *comes*, *vicarius*, or *centenarius*. It was, moreover, final; for, as one of the Capitularies distinctly says, "After the *scabini* have condemned a man as a robber, it is not lawful for either the *comes* or the *vicarius* to grant him life."

The *scabini* were expected to be present at the meetings of the county—probably also, to some extent, at those of the nation, and they joined in the assent which was there given to any new Capitularies that were promulgated by the emperor. It is easy to see how, both in their judicial and in their legislative capacity, the *scabini* may have acted as a useful check on the lawless encroachments of the counts. There was probably in this institution a germ which, had the emperors remained mighty, would have limited the power of the aristocracy, and have formed in time a democratic basis upon which a strong and stable monarchy might have been erected.

IV. Lastly, a few words must be said as to the permanent results of Charles's life and work on the state-system of Europe. In endeavouring to appraise them let us keep our minds open to the consideration not only of that which actually was, but also of that which might have been, had the descendants of Charles been as able men as himself and his progenitors.

The three great political events of Charles's reign were his conquest of Italy, his consolidation of the Frankish kingdom, and his assumption of the imperial title.

1. His conduct towards the vanquished Lombards was, on the whole, generous and statesmanlike. By assuming the title of King of the Lombards he showed that it was not his object to destroy the nationality of the countrymen of Alboin, nor to fuse them into one people with the Franks. Had his son Pippin lived and transmitted his sceptre to his descendants, there might possibly have been founded a kingdom of Italy, strong, patriotic, and enduring. In that event some of the glorious fruits of art and literature which were ripened in the independent Italian republics of the Middle Ages might never have been brought forth, but the Italians, though a less artistic people, would have been spared much bloodshed and many despairs.

But we can only say that this was a possible contingency. By the policy (inherited from his father) which he pursued towards the papal see, Charles called into existence a power which would probably always have been fatal to the unity and freedom of Italy. That wedge of Church-Dominions thrust in between the north and south would always tend to keep Lombardy and Tuscany apart from Spoleto and Benevento; and the endless wrangle between Pope and King would perhaps have been renewed even as in the days of the Lombards. The descendants of the pacific and

God-crowned king would then have become the "un-utterable" and the "not-to-be-mentioned" Franks, and peace and unity would have been as far from the fated land as they have been in very deed for a thousand years.

2. Charles's greatest work, as has been once or twice hinted in the course of the preceding narrative, was his extension and consolidation of the Frankish kingdom. One cannot see that he did much for what we now call France, but his work east of the Rhine was splendidly successful. Converting the Saxons,—a triumph of civilisation, however barbarous were the methods employed,—subduing the rebellious Bavarians, keeping the Danes and the Sclavonic tribes on his eastern border in check, and utterly crushing the Avars, he gave the Teutonic race that position of supremacy in Central Europe which, whatever may have been the ebb and flow of Teutonism in later centuries, it has never been forced to surrender, and which, with all its faults, has been a blessing to Europe.

3. As to the assumption of the imperial title, it is much more difficult to speak with confidence. We have seen reason to think that Charles himself was only half persuaded of its expediency. It was a noble idea, this revival of the old world-wide empire and its conversion into a *Civitas Dei*, the realised dream of St. Augustine. But none knew better than the monarch himself how far his empire came short of these grand prophetic visions; and profounder scholars than Alcuin could have told him how little it had really in common with the state which was ruled by Augustus or by Trajan. That empire had sprung out of a democratic republic, and retained for centuries something of that resistless

energy which the consciousness of self-government gives to a brave and patient people. Charles's empire was cradled, not in the city but in the forest; its essential principle was the loyalty of henchmen to their chief; it was already permeated by the spirit of feudalism, and between feudalism and any true reproduction of the *Imperium Romanum* there could be no abiding union.

I need not here allude to the divergence in language, customs, and modes of thought between the various nationalities which composed the emperor's dominions. The mutual antagonism of nations and languages was not so strong in the Middle Ages as it has been in our own day, and possibly a succession of able rulers might have kept the two peoples, who in their utterly different languages swore in 842 the great oath of Strasburg, still one. But the spirit of feudalism was more fatal to the unity of the empire than these differences of race and language. The mediæval emperor was perpetually finding himself overtopped by one or other of his nominal vassals, and history has few more pitiable spectacles than some that were presented by the rulers of the Holy Roman Empire—men bearing the great names of Cæsar and Augustus—tossed helplessly to and fro on the waves of European politics, the laughing-stock of their own barons and marquises, and often unable to provide for the ordinary expenses of their households.

But all this belongs to the story of the Middle Ages, not to the life of the founder of the empire. It would be absurd to say that he could have foreseen all the weak points of the great, and on the whole beneficent, institution which he bestowed on Western Europe. And whatever estimate we may form of the good or the evil which resulted from the great event of the eight hundredth Christmas day, none will deny that the whole history of Europe for at least seven hundred years was profoundly modified by the life and mighty deeds of Charles the Great.

NOTE

ON THE ENTOMBMENT OF CHARLEMAGNE

A CURIOUS and somewhat difficult question arises as to the disposal of the remains of the great emperor. The account given in the text [1] rests on the authority of Einhard, and is fully confirmed by Thegan the biographer of Louis the Pious. But in the year 1000 the Emperor Otho III. opened the tomb in the presence of two bishops, and a knight named Otho of Lomello, and according to the statement of that knight communicated to the author of the chronicle of Novalese, they found the emperor sitting on a throne with a golden crown on his head, and holding a golden sceptre in his hands. The hands were covered with gloves, through which the nails protruding had worked their way. A little chapel (*tuguriolum*) of marble and lime was erected over him, through the roof of which the excavators made their way. None of the emperor's limbs had rotted away, but a little piece had fallen from the end of the nose, which Otho caused to be replaced in gold. The four discoverers fell on their knees before the majestic figure. Then they clothed him with white robes, cut the finger nails, took away one tooth as a relic, closed the roof of the chapel and departed.

The account is a very circumstantial one, and is given by a contemporary chronicler on the authority of one of the actors of the scene who is a fairly well-known historical personage. Yet most modern enquirers accept the conclusion advocated by Theodor Lindner (Die Fabel von der Bestattung Karls des Grossen), that the story must be

[1] Page 231.

rejected as untrue, in other words, that Otho of Lomello in
relating it was playing on the credulity of his hearers. The
chief reasons for this conclusion are, that the story is hope-
lessly at variance with the statements of Einhard and Thegan.
If the body was buried on the very day of death, there would
be no time for the elaborate process of embalming which
this story requires. The words of the epitaph "humatum,"
"sub hoc conditorio situm est," would not be applicable to
such a mode of interment. Moreover, such a very unusual mode
of dealing with the great emperor's body would surely have
attracted some notice from the ninth-century authors who
in prose and verse celebrate the deeds of Charles, not one of
whom makes the slightest allusion to it. Lastly, though an
industrious search has been often made, no one has ever been
able to find a trace of the *tuguriolum* (necessarily a room of a
certain size) in which the corpse was said to have been seated.

In 1165, at the time of the canonisation of Charles, his body
was taken up by the Emperor Frederick Barbarossa, removed
from the marble sarcophagus, in which it had lain for nearly
352 years, and placed in a wooden coffer in the middle of the
church. For this wooden coffer was substituted fifty years
later, at the order of Frederick II., a costly shrine adorned
with gold and jewels in which at the present day, every
six years, the relics of "St. Charles the Great," are exhibited
to the people. The head is separated from the body and
enclosed in a silver portrait-bust of fourteenth - century
workmanship.

APPENDIX A

GENEALOGY OF THE ANCESTORS OF CHARLES THE GREAT

St. Arnulf, 582-640;
Bishop of Metz, 612-627 (?)

Pippin "of Lan- = Itta (?)
din," 585-639. 591-651.

Chlodulf, 599-696;
Bishop of Metz, 656-696.

Adelgisel or Anse-
gisel, 605-685 (?)

Becga
615-694.

Grimwald
†658.

Gertrude, Abbess of
Nivelles, 625-659.

Childebert proclaimed king
by his father, 657.

=

Pippin "of Heris-
tal," 631-714.

= Alphaida

Plectrudis =

Grimwald, †714.

Theudwald.

Drogo, †708.

Hrotrudis=Charles Martel, 686-741. = Swanahild.

Grifo, †753.

Carloman, 713-755 ; abdicated 747.

PIPPIN I., b. 714 ; crowned 752, †768. = Bertrada, †783.

CHARLES the Great, b. 742 (?), king 768
Emperor 800, †814.

CARLOMAN, b. 751,
king 768, †771.

Note.—Many of the above dates are conjectural.

APPENDIX B

FAMILY OF ST. CHARLES THE GREAT

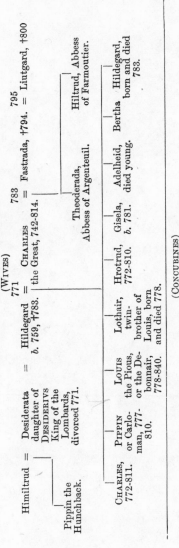
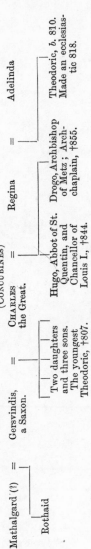

(WIVES)

Himiltrud =   Desiderata, daughter of DESIDERIVS King of the Lombards, divorced 771.

771   Hildegard =   783   795
b. 759, †783.   CHARLES = Fastrada, †794. = Liutgard, †800
the Great, 742-814.

Pippin the Hunchback.

CHARLES, 772-811.

PIPPIN or Carloman, 777-810.

LOUIS the Pious, or the Debonnair, 778-840.

Lothair, twin-brother of Louis, born and died 778.

Hrotrud, 772-810.

Gisela, *b.* 781.

Adelheid, died young.

Bertha

Hildegard, born and died 783.

Theoderada, Abbess of Argenteuil.

Hiltrud, Abbess of Farmoutier.

(CONCUBINES)

CHARLES the Great.

Mathalgard (?) =

Gersvindis, a Saxon. =

= Regina

= Adelinda

Rothaid

Two daughters and three sons. The youngest Theodoric, †807.

Hugo, Abbot of St. Quentin, and Chancellor of Louis I, †844.

Drogo, Archbishop of Metz; Arch-chaplain, †855.

Theodoric, *b.* 810. Made an ecclesiastic 818.

082322